THE GENERALS
THE NEW AMERICAN HEROES

"I'm not one of these right-wing military conservatives who says the greatest day of my life was when I went to war. In a lot of ways I am a pacifist. But I know what war is. I am certainly antiwar. But I also believe there are things worth fighting for."

General H. Norman Schwarzkopf

"Yes, I climbed, and I climbed well, and I climbed hard, and I climbed over the cliff, but always on the backs and the contributions of those who went before. Now, on the top of that cliff and looking ahead, there are still more rivers to be crossed."

General Colin L. Powell

THE
GENERALS
THE NEW AMERICAN HEROES

BILL ADLER

AVON BOOKS ◆ NEW YORK

THE GENERALS: THE NEW AMERICAN HEROES is an original publication of Avon Books. This work has never appeared in book form.

AVON BOOKS
A division of
The Hearst Corporation
105 Madison Avenue
New York, New York 10016

First Avon Books Printing: June 1991

AVON TRADEMARK REG. U.S. PAT. OFF. AND IN OTHER COUNTRIES, MARCA REGISTRADA, HECHO EN U.S.A.

Printed in the U.S.A.

RA 10 9 8 7 6 5 4 3 2 1

Contents

1

Meeting in the Desert

The two generals sat side by side, rigged out in colorful desert camouflage, looking relaxed and calm, as if they might have been candidly caught exchanging jovial war experiences with each other. It was a classic photo opportunity for the world press. And the world press made the most of it.

The pictures circulated almost instantly all over the world quite soon after they were taken.

For, more than anyone else—perhaps even more than the Commander in Chief of the armed services, President George Bush—these two men were responsible for the detailed day-to-day movements of the battle plan code-named Operation Desert Storm. In plainer, simpler words—the war to liberate Kuwait from Iraqi occupation.

In the pictures, the general on the left had the name POW-ELL sewed to his right breast, and the other the name SCHWARZKOPF on his. Powell was Mr. Inside, and Schwarzkopf Mr. Outside. Powell, Chairman of the Joint Chiefs of Staff, ran the Pentagon and acted as liaison between the armed services and the White House. Schwarzkopf, commander of Operation Desert Storm, was in charge of all the troops and matériel in the Persian Gulf area; he was the man responsible for everything that happened in the field of what had become the war zone.

In the pictures from that photo opportunity, which occurred on Saturday, February 9, 1991, in General H. Norman Schwarzkopf's underground headquarters near Riyadh, Saudi

Arabia, their relaxed attitudes belied the seriousness of their meeting. That meeting was crucial to the future conduct of the war that was raging north of them, and had been raging in the air for four weeks already.

General Schwarzkopf had opened the war with these fighting words:

"I have seen in your eyes a fire of determination to get this war done quickly. My confidence in you is total. Our cause is just. Now, you must be the thunder and the lightning of Desert Storm."

President Bush added his words:

"This will *not* be another Vietnam. Our troops will not be asked to fight with one hand tied behind their back."

Saddam Hussein, Iraq's war leader, spoke to his people and to the world in these words:

"The great duel, the mother of all battles, has begun."

Prior to August 1990 there were very few people in the world—very few even in the United States—who had ever heard of two four-star generals named Powell and Schwarzkopf.

In August, Schwarzkopf had surfaced in a press conference held in his Riyadh headquarters, to be quoted in the world press about Operation Desert Shield, a buildup of troops and matériel in Saudi Arabia aimed at preventing Iraqi troops in Kuwait from attacking and seizing the oil fields to the south.

Powell did not make his initial appearance until the opening of the war itself—Operation Desert Storm—on January 16, 1990.

When they did face the assembled media, these two men achieved instant international celebrity, becoming world figures overnight and commanding the attention and adulation of millions and millions of people.

Ironically enough, both men were born within three years of each other in the darkest years of the Depression in the 1930s. But there almost any similarity vanished. One came up the hard way; the other came up the even *harder* way.

First, the one who came up the hard way.

H. Norman Schwarzkopf could never have hoped to be anything but right out in the front of every group in which he was included. In physique an enormous man, described variously as anything from six feet two to six feet five (he's supposed to be six-three and a half), he always managed to bring down upon himself instant judgments and assessments of his worth—some positive, some (probably more) negative.

One of the most jeering comments on his personality was the nickname he had been saddled with during his early Vietnam years—"Stormin' Norman." Later he told Barbara Walters why he disliked being called that.

" 'Stormin' Norman' tends to portray someone who just goes around and raises hell all the time and just kicks everybody around and has no sensitivity at all. . . . That's why I don't like it. I have a temper. I will freely admit to that. I'm not proud of it. I don't like myself when I lose my temper. But I . . . wear my heart squarely on my sleeve. I believe I owe it to everyone to let them know when I don't like something. But I don't carry a grudge. I do not browbeat my staff. I do not drive people into the ground. I am not a total martinet. I am a human being, and 'Stormin' Norman' portrays something that's . . . mad all the time and raising hell all the time, and that's . . . not me."

What name did he like?

"The Bear," he replied, admitting it was an ambiguous nickname, but perhaps that was its charm. "Sometimes I'm a teddy bear. Sometimes I'm a grizzly bear. Sometimes I'm a polar bear, sometimes I'm a panda bear, sometimes I'm a koala bear."

On the subject of animals, he was once asked if he was a hawk or a dove. "Neither," Schwarzkopf replied. "I'm an owl. I hope to watch, to learn, and be wise."

One personality element of Schwarzkopf's belies the owl simile exemplified by the old nursery rhyme:

> A wise old owl sat in an oak.
> The more he heard, the less he spoke.
> The less he spoke, the more he heard.
> I wish I were that wise old bird.

H. Norman Schwarzkopf has never been a man to keep his mouth closed—not when something springs to mind that he feels should be said.

All of which leads back to the "Stormin' Norman" sobriquet and how he got it. One West Point graduate, a retired officer who knew him at the Academy, said: "He always had the reputation of being a bit of a screamer, very hard on the staff, very impulsive."

Other uncomplimentary assessments include that of Christopher Hitchens, who reported on H. Norman Schwarzkopf for *The Nation*:

"I saw the low-comedy figure of Gen. H. Norman Schwarzkopf Jr. swim onto my screen the other day, talking out of the side of his mouth about 'kicking the butt' of Saddam Hussein and beaming at the puerile appellation 'Stormin' Norman.'" The identification of Schwarzkopf as a "low-comedy figure" indicated clearly where *he* was coming from.

In *The Progressive*, Linda Rocawich wrote: "General Schwarzkopf . . . was deputy commander of the U.S. invasion of Grenada in October 1983, a brilliant public-relations success that actually bore a fair resemblance to a Keystone Cops routine." A Defense Department assessment of the invasion, she reported, concluded with these words: "An almost total lack of intelligence data about the situation on the island . . . was followed by critical failures of military communication and faulty tactics."

"If we go to war in the Persian Gulf," she wrote in January 1991, "everyone agrees it will take longer than two or three days and we will lose vastly more than twenty or thirty lives, even with the best of planning and execution. But this [Schwarzkopf] is one of the men who planned and executed the Grenada operation. What has he learned in seven years?"

A "military source" quoted by Linda Diebel in the *Toronto Star* said: "I never liked him. He's a bombastic asshole. He always tended to open his mouth when he should have engaged his brain."

Retired Admiral Joseph Metcalf, who commanded the Grenada invasion, recently told *Army Times*: "He's a good guy to go to war with because he's a good solid commander. He's a soldier; he's more comfortable out with the troops than he is in the Pentagon.''

And General Colin L. Powell said of Schwarzkopf that he was ''a statesman who understands the political and diplomatic dimensions of a national security issue.''

''Look,'' Schwarzkopf said about himself, ''I'm not one of these right-wing military conservatives who says the greatest day of my life was when I went to war. In a lot of ways I am a pacifist—though that might be too strong a word. But I know what war is. I am certainly antiwar. But I also believe these are things worth fighting for.''

From his experiences in Vietnam, Schwarzkopf became agonizingly sensitive about the loss of men—hardly the image of the gung-ho military commander who blows men away to win stars.

''Every waking and sleeping moment, my nightmare is the fact that I will give an order that will cause countless numbers of human beings to lose their lives. I don't want my troops to die. I don't want my troops to be maimed. It's an intensely personal, an emotional thing for me. Any decision you have to make that involves the loss of human life is nothing you do lightly. I agonize over it.''

C. D. B. Bryan, who interviewed Schwarzkopf extensively for research on his book, *Friendly Fire*, commented about Schwarzkopf's quotation above:

''I believe him.''

What's the real truth about this man?

It probably lurks somewhere midway between pro and con. But it was in the cards that Schwarzkopf would always land somewhere where conflict and controversy would swirl about him.

The same was never true of Colin Luther Powell.

Whereas Schwarzkopf was hot-tempered and outgoing, Powell was always cool and introspective. Before being tapped to be Chairman of the Joint Chiefs of Staff under President Bush, Powell served the White House in the capacity of Deputy Secretary of Defense—and later National Security Adviser.

When he was appointed to the latter post, Marlin Fitzwater, the chief White House spokesman under President Ronald

Reagan, said: "We have no concerns about [Powell's] dedication, his objectivity, and his ability to deal with all the agencies of government, civilian and military, in a fair and objective fashion."

A close friend of Powell's who detested the Reagan administration but liked Powell put it this way: "Colin is careful, honest, professional, and cautious. He believes in the art of the possible. He stood out among the Reagan people because of this quality."

Another friend described Powell this way: "His essential quality is that he is a total family man. He works very hard at his family. He works very hard at his job."

From the start, Powell had the Washingtonian touch, that quality that separates the movers and shakers from the drones—the ability to rise above the twists and turns of the moment and survive. Flavor-of-the-month Washington, much like Hollywood, can point its fickle finger to a new rising star at the drop of a hat, and fame can be snatched instantly even from the likes of a Powell.

In fact, Powell did make enemies in the Pentagon, men who branded him as a "desk jockey" who got to the top because of political connections and behind-the-scenes manipulation and not because of command expertise. In spite of these enemies, there was no denying that Powell had an uncanny knack of being able to get along with just about everybody, which is always part and parcel of being an instinctive political animal.

But sometimes even his best friends . . .

There was Jesse Jackson, who could not hold his tongue about Powell's excellent relationship with President Reagan, who Jesse Jackson thought had a poor civil rights record. This prompted Jackson to attack Powell as a man who would never be "a popular hero among blacks."

For once, the cool Powell warmed up and took issue with Jackson's rebuke. "Surprisingly, most black American groups I talk to are proud of the fact that I have this job," he told Jackson. "The fact that I have the job is to the credit of the President. . . . He knew me and he gave it to me."

Despite this occasional sideswipe at Jackson, Powell always

held Jackson in high esteem for his bid for the presidency, even though Jackson was a Democrat and Powell served under two Republican administrations.

Powell's shining career as National Security Adviser was capped off by the presentation of the Distinguished Service Award by Secretary of State George Shultz for Powell's work on the U.S.-Soviet arms control agreement and the Moscow summit.

Shultz cited Powell for his "consummate skill and coordination of U.S. policy, which contributed indispensably to the ratification of the U.S.-Soviet treaty on the elimination of intermediate-range and shorter-range missiles and the success of the Moscow summit."

Frank Carlucci, Powell's immediate boss, said about Powell: "Nobody could provide you with better guidance in this building or in the United States government. He is extraordinarily bright, articulate, and with excellent judgment."

Caspar Weinberger had been impressed with Powell as early as 1972, when Powell was a White House Fellow assigned to work at the Office of Management and Budget, where Weinberger was the director.

"He is . . . a particularly effective administrator-manager who anticipates and prepares for the various twists and turns events can take," Weinberger said. "[He] is one of the very best persons I have ever worked with in any of the positions I've had. He has excelled in everything he has touched, and he always will. I don't think you can find anyone who has anything bad to say about Colin Powell, which is an extraordinary thing when you've been around Washington as long as he has—in highly sensitive and vital assignments."

None other than Britain's main foreign policy adviser to then Prime Minister Margaret Thatcher, Charles Powell, claimed that he had never encountered an American military man more impressive than Colin L. Powell.

During his service as senior military assistant to Secretary of Defense Caspar Weinberger, Powell lasted three whole years in the position. What became evident about Powell during this long (by government standards) stint with Weinberger was that he had a definite flair for being able to get along with virtually everybody he had to work with. From his associates he earned a reputation for "being more of an expediter than a global thinker." And that, considering the parameters within which it was uttered, was the most telling comment of all.

In no way does Powell seem to be the enigma that Schwarzkopf was and is. And yet, of course, there are elements buried in Powell's persona that do not always come out when he is, say, on the lecture circuit, speaking and generally forming political policy decisions for the White House and the Pentagon.

Two men. Two generals. Two different personalities. How did they work together?

This meeting in the desert that the two generals were holding was an extremely important one. In order to understand more clearly the precise nature of the "details" the generals were discussing, it might be well to backtrack a bit on the course of Operation Desert Storm, the war in the Persian Gulf, and examine the details of what led up to a *need* for such a meeting.

The war between the Coalition Forces and Iraq began just before 3 a.m., Persian Gulf time, on the morning of January 16, 1991, some hours after a prearranged "deadline" of January 15 had passed without the proper withdrawal of Iraqi troops from occupied Kuwait.

A Tomahawk cruise missile from the deck of the USS *Wisconsin* slammed through the air in a northerly direction toward Baghdad. After it more Tomahawks followed, along with missiles by the dozens. Soon the night sky was ablaze with bursts of light and searing trails of fire.

Coordinated with these missile attacks, the U.S. Air Force flew off in low-altitude attacks in the early dawn, sending down "smart" bombs to target in on command and control centers used by the Iraqi army. Only a handful of Iraqi pilots rose to the challenge, and most of them were blown out of the sky.

Simultaneously with the opening of what was later described as the "air war," Iraq launched a Scud missile attack on Israel with eight missiles striking Tel Aviv, Haifa, and Ramallah. It was during the first hours of the war that the untested ability of the Patriot antimissile missile was established for good when one destroyed a Scud sent toward Riyadh. Patriots were immediately sent to Israel with American teams to man them.

During the first week of the war, the U.S. made some 10,000 air sorties over Iraq—that is, 10,000 flights over Iraqi terrain.

The Iraqis took several prisoners of war, and were careful to parade them triumphantly in front of television cameras to show the world that the Americans were helpless in the face of Iraq's brave troops. The POWs, some showing marks of what could have been beatings, were forced to read statements obviously written by their captors in a kind of propaganda jargon that fooled absolutely no one who heard them.

In another war action, the Iraqis dumped millions of barrels of oil into the Persian Gulf, where it spread in a huge slick thirty-five miles long, killing birds, fish, and other marine animals. It even threatened the Saudi desalinization plants along the coast. American F-111s bombed the supertanker terminal pipes where the flow was emanating from and stopped the discharge.

In Washington, General Colin L. Powell, Chairman of the Joint Chiefs of Staff, reassured Americans in a television briefing that the war had not turned sour just because Saddam Hussein was still alive. The focus of the bombing shifted, aiming at troops and supply lines. A large number of Iraq's jets flew to Iran.

By the end of the second week, Coalition Forces had flown a total of 27,000 sorties.

During the third week of the war, ground "probes" were made by Iraqi forces from Khafji to Umm Hujul, along about fifty miles of the Saudi-Kuwaiti border. Coalition Forces turned them back, helped by air support. What little there was left of the Iraqi navy was also put out of business. Over 47,000 sorties had been logged by the third week of the war.

Now, during the fourth week of the war, came the time to assess the situation. There was little doubt that the Coalition Forces of the United Nations were in control of the air. Iraqi jets were flying to Iran; trickles of Iraqi deserters were flowing into U.S. hands.

It was time for the so-called ground war to begin. All along it had been hoped that air power would be sufficient to draw

Saddam Hussein out in the open to wave a white flag. He had not budged from his bunker. There was no sign of capitulation. Phase two of Operation Desert Storm was in the offing.

But Congress was getting jumpy. Would the world look at the U.S. as an enormous bully subjecting a tiny country to merciless destruction—for *oil*? The word went up the line to Secretary of Defense Dick Cheney and Joint Chiefs Chairman Powell: hold up on the proposed ground war for a bit. Maybe, Congress thought, something could be worked out *politically* to make the Iraqis pull out of Kuwait.

It was during this period that President Bush instructed Cheney and Powell to fly to Saudi Arabia for consultation with Schwarzkopf and Coalition commanders for a final assessment before setting the date of a ground offensive.

At this point over 65,000 air sorties had been flown in the devastating air offensive of the Coalition Forces.

What happened in Riyadh headquarters between the two generals during their discussion of the coming ground war was top secret. What they said in public afterward, of course, could have conveyed or could not have conveyed what they said in private.

For example, Powell was quoted later as saying that the ground assault would be part of a seamless plan. "It is a single, integrated campaign. The air campaign will never end."

He noted that casualties in any ground war could be very heavy. He added that Saddam Hussein had designed a war that would create a large number of casualties. However, Powell said, that kind of war might not actually follow, and astronomical figures in body count might not materialize at all.

"[That may not necessarily be] the way such a war would be fought." To clarify that, "The assumption is that a ground campaign is Mr. Hussein's campaign. [The assumption that] we'll fight it this way is not necessarily an accurate one."

No?

Schwarzkopf was interviewed on ABC News the night of his meeting with Powell, and he said it was too soon to say whether a ground assault would be necessary to free Kuwait or not. The implication was that a ground war was not in the cards at that moment.

No?

Whatever all this rhetoric proved or did not prove, the fact that the meeting of these two top military men—representing the Pentagon and the field of battle—had taken place at all initiated a spate of comments from politicians and statesmen all over the world.

In France, President Francois Mitterrand offered *his* impression that a ground assault was inevitable.

"It will be fought," he announced to his fellow compatriots on television, but he predicted that the war would last no longer than spring. He promised that French forces would not use chemical or biological weapons.

The objective of the war, he said, was to liberate Kuwait, not to destroy Iraq's war machine. However, he said that what the Coalition Forces were now seeing of the immense Iraqi military machine indicated that "if we had not fought this war now, we would have had to fight a bigger war in two or four years."

He noted that any postwar settlement should include international conferences to resolve the Palestinian and Lebanon situations.

The commander of British forces in the Persian Gulf—Lieutenant General Sir Peter de la Billiere—said that there was really nothing that could spare the Coalition Forces a bloody ground battle.

"This is a personal opinion," he explained. "I believe a land war is inevitable. Saddam Hussein is a man who uses human life as a currency to buy what he wants in this world." He also said that Hussein "is quite deliberately deploying his weapons among civilians with the precise aim of killing civilians"—obviously for the value of the propaganda such killings elicited in the world press.

"We're now moving into the next phase of this war," he continued, "toward the most difficult and certainly the final phase. The bombing they've already been subjected to is minor compared to what they've got coming." He pointed out that the bombing might continue for weeks before Coalition Forces moved forward.

When Cheney and Powell returned to the United States on

Sunday, February 10, they reported directly to the President their confidential findings on the state of the armed forces. No action was taken immediately.

On February 20, just as the sixth week of fighting began, Baghdad radio, in the person of Latif Nusayyif Jasim, the Minister of Culture and Information, unloaded on General H. Norman Schwarzkopf. The diatribe was supposedly a "comment" about remarks made by Schwarzkopf in Najd and Hijaz.

"Every day," the radio report said, "one of the criminals of the U.S.-Zionist aggression against Iraq and the Arab nation makes statements in which he tries to patch up the psychological condition of the aggressive forces in an attempt to help them hold out in the confrontation with the valiant, victorious forces.

"This person, Schwarzkopf, commander of the U.S. forces, following at the heel of the clique of the war criminal George Bush, makes statements to this or that paper. The most recent product of his rotten brain is his statement to the *Los Angeles [Times]* in which he said that Iraq is being, as he alleges, exhausted.

"However, this damned person hastily tries to correct himself by listing indisputable facts about our valiant Iraqi armed forces. Thus, scrapping his first idea, he says that the Iraqis' capability must not be underestimated. Thus, the criminal of aggression, Schwarzkopf, adds a new blunder to the blunders of his criminal clique."

And so on and so forth. It was only a foreshadowing of worse to come. Things were heating up for Saddam Hussein. And in the middle of the week he moved—not toward his enemies, but toward Mikhail Gorbachev. Gorbachev immediately announced to the Coalition Forces that Iraq wanted a cease-fire . . . but there were so many conditions that it seemed ridiculous. President Bush said so.

It was on the following Thursday, in the sixth week of fighting, that a crucial meeting of the war cabinet took place in the White House. Joint Chiefs Chairman Colin L. Powell was wearing a green turtleneck and a sports jacket. Vice President Dan Quayle and Defense Secretary Dick Cheney came in tuxedos, having just returned from dinner with visiting Queen Margrethe II of Denmark. The Iraqi "withdrawal" was still on the front burner, but it was obviously not coming to a fruitful boil. It was definitely "unacceptable," as one typed sheet in front of each cabinet member had it.

In fact, there were two sheets: one a list of "criteria" by which the allies would decide whether the withdrawal was unconditional and worthy of a cease-fire; and the second a single-page argument that the Gorbachev-Aziz agreement was "unacceptable."

The President spoke. "I like both of these. Let's put them together. It's not enough to just say we don't accept the Soviet plan." He explained that he had been on the phone with Gorbachev and had told him why it was unacceptable. "We ought to lay them out to the whole world."

Powell nodded. He wanted to get a move on. "Well, let's set a date and set a time." He was talking about the ground war, the second phase of battle.

"I think that's a good idea," Bush agreed.

The deadline, Powell said, would be "helpful to the military because then my guys in the field know what to expect. They know exactly what to be looking for and when."

The discussions ranged over the timing: Sunday? Monday? When?

Powell opted for a date as soon as possible. Bush was with him. Secretary of State James Baker cautioned that the ultimatum must have Coalition support and must seem to allow a reasonable time for Iraqi acceptance.

"The diplomatic question was the toughest," a participant later explained. "We had twenty-eight partners, and the biggest concern was making sure we would get everyone on board."

Saturday? someone suggested.

"I think that's a good idea," Bush said. "What's it do for you, Colin?"

"It's good for me."

"What's it do for you, Jim?"

The Secretary of State said, "It's good for me too, but it is a new item that the allies don't know about and we need to get back to them about.''

"Okay. We're agreed, then. It's noon Saturday," Bush said. And that was exactly what it was to be.

Just as Powell and Schwarzkopf had agreed.

2

Powell:
The Ghetto Warrior

Like Ronald Reagan, Colin Powell was never much of a student when he was in school. Perhaps that was the reason the two men got along so well years later when they worked in the White House together.

As a fifth grader in P.S. 39 in the Bronx, Powell studied in the "slow" class. In Morris High School in the Hunts Point section of the South Bronx, all he could manage was Cs. At City College of New York he majored in geology only because he thought it was easy. It was obvious from the beginning that Powell was not fated to lead a life in academia.

When he joined the ROTC program at City College, he got an A. He decided that he was finally on the right road; he was right. The military was a road that would lead him to the chairmanship of the Joint Chiefs of Staff. And maybe even higher.

Colin Luther Powell was born in Harlem in New York City on April 5, 1937. His father, Luther Theopolis Powell, was a shipping clerk in Manhattan's garment district. His mother, Maud Ariel McKoy Powell, was a seamstress.

Powell's parents emigrated from Jamaica by way of Panama twenty-odd years before their son was born. Their roots in Jamaica might have had something to do with naming their son "Colin"—a typically British name.

From his early years, Colin Powell had trouble with the pronunciation of his first name. Was it KAH-lin or KOH-lin? In the United States, the name was for some reason pronounced "KOH-lin," whereas in Britain, "KAH-lin."

"My parents named me KAH-lin," he said. "My parents were British subjects [in Jamaica] and they knew how the name should be pronounced."

But not in America. "When I was a young boy," Powell remembered, "there was a famous American war hero at the beginning of World War II by the name of KOH-lin Kelly— I think that is an Irish pronunciation, I am not entirely sure— but my friends in the street, hearing that he had pronounced his name KOH-lin, started calling me KOH-lin."

He grew accustomed to KOH-lin and came to prefer it, since he was usually called that, "much to the regret of my British friends, who consider us a bunch of ignorant Americans for mispronouncing the name."

Colin P. Kelly, Jr., became a war hero of World War II when he was shot down after bombing a Japanese battleship. In a posthumous award, President Franklin Roosevelt wrote a letter to "a future President" asking that the hero's son, Colin P. Kelly III, be given an appointment to West Point when he came of age.

"The young man did grow up, did want to go to West Point," Powell said, "went to West Point and into the army. He served in Vietnam as an armor officer, came back from Vietnam and went into the chaplaincy and became an Episcopal priest.

"I met him when he was a lieutenant colonel and I was a brigadier general, and I said, 'What's your name?' He said, 'KOH-lin Kelly.' And I said, 'Thank God, you have been mispronouncing your name all your life just as I have.'"

His British name notwithstanding, Powell grew up in typical urban fashion, but with one slight difference. Being Jamaican, his parents inculcated in him the importance of education and personal achievement. They demanded that their children— Colin had an older sister, Marilyn—"do something with [their] lives."

Powell grew up preferring to crop his hair short, which he

felt molded his light brown complexion most smoothly. He had a big, wide, unlined, carefree face in his youth, and it did not change much as he grew older. He always had a good solid build. He would grow up to be six feet one inch tall, and weigh about two hundred muscular pounds.

This self-confessed "ghetto warrior," who nevertheless idolized Martin Luther King, Jr., all his life, determined to grow up dedicated to the concept of nonviolence. There was that singular lack of a chip on the shoulder. He never felt that he was being discriminated against when he was young.

As he once put it, "I grew up in a neighborhood where everybody was a minority—blacks, Jews, Puerto Ricans—and I never thought there was something wrong with me because I was black."

He grew up to tell black schoolchildren, "My color is somebody else's problem and not mine. You just take me as I am."

Yet he always deplored the rampant racism in America that he encountered later on in his life. In fact, it became the only bone that he learned to pick with the country in which he was born. In Jamaica, he has said, his parents never felt that they were inferior to anyone else—even whites—in that British Commonwealth.

Powell grew to believe that there was a reason, perhaps, that West Indian immigrant blacks made out better than other blacks in America. It was, he thought, the fact that in West India "there is something of a tradition of a British education."

According to his lights, "Jamaicans and other West Indians were never oppressed to the extent that Southern blacks were. Southern blacks were raised believing that they were inferior. . . . West Indians did not arrive in the United States thinking that way and, for the most part, they lived in the North, where it was different."

Powell came from a family of high achievers. One of his well-known cousins is Bruce Llewellyn, the first black to preside over the Federal Overseas Private Investment Corporation. He also co-owns the Philadelphia Coca-Cola Bottling Works and chairs the black-owned TV station, WKBW, in Buffalo, New York.

Another of Powell's cousins is Judge James (Skiz) Watson,

who works for the U.S. Court of International Trade. Powell's cousin Dorothy Cropper works for the New York Court of Claims. Ambassador Arthur Lewis, erstwhile U.S. ambassador to Sierra Leone, is also one of Powell's cousins.

When Powell was born, his parents were living in Harlem. A few years later Colin, his sister, Marilyn, older than he by five and a half years, and their parents moved to the "better" address of 952 Kelly Street in the South Bronx.

Their four-bedroom apartment has long since been demolished. That address, now a crime-ridden jungle, got national renown in 1981 when Hollywood made a movie about the area called *Fort Apache: The Bronx*. Directed by Daniel Petrie, it starred Paul Newman and was well received by the critics. The title tells it all.

When Powell was living there, however, he found the place idyllic. So did his sister, who grew up to become a bilingual teacher of advanced primary school students in Santa Ana, California.

"The neighborhood was like a small town," she once described it. "Everybody looked out for each other. We could never get into trouble. Everywhere you went there were forty pairs of eyes watching you."

Powell said that while living there he "didn't know what a 'majority' was," let alone a "minority." "You were either black, Puerto Rican, Jewish, or of some strange European extraction," he wrote in his alumni magazine.

He worshipped the ground his parents walked on. If anything, he respected them even more as he grew up. "More, as I get older, I continue to have greater and greater affection for my parents, what they did that I didn't know that they were doing."

Powell claimed that books were an integral part of his early life. That, despite the fact that he never got straight As in school; his grades, to put it mildly, were unspectacular. His sister, Marilyn, always remembered how lighthearted he was about his studies. Lighthearted, perhaps, or downright noncaring.

"I was the one who was always asking our mother to read street signs to me and spell words when I was little when she was taking me out for a walk," she recalled. "Colin could not have cared less."

Many years later, when her brother was appointed Chairman of the Joint Chiefs of Staff, Marilyn Powell smiled ruefully. "Look at us now. I guess he was a late bloomer."

Powell's parents belonged to the Anglican and Episcopal churches and devoted themselves to bringing up their children. According to Powell, the Anglican religion of the West Indies was "high church," for it emphasized ritual and the burning of incense, similar to the Roman Catholic religion. In New York, Powell attended St. Margaret's Episcopal Church on 151st Street.

Waxing sentimental, he once said of his parents that they were "the kind of family that in a very quiet, nonpreachy way laid out expectations for the children, for all the cousins and the extended family."

He added, pounding like a politician on the stump, "When you saw both of your parents work, you saw them sacrifice, and when the weekends came and we had time, the whole family got together. Somehow over time, they made it clear to all of us, my sister and myself as well as the extended family of cousins, that there were certain expectations built into the family system."

He felt that his family was partly responsible for his success in life. "You realized that those modestly educated immigrants were not doing all of this for themselves; they were doing all of this for you. So it was unthinkable in the family not to do something. Doing it didn't mean becoming a brain surgeon. It just meant getting educated, getting a job, and going as far as you could with that job."

This has turned out to be Powell's version of the Mom-Dad-and-Apple-Pie speech.

Powell's parents never finished high school. That did not mean that they did not believe in hard work. Powell once said, "There was something of a tradition of hard work being the way to succeed. And there was simply an expectation that existed in the family—you were supposed to do better. And it was a bloody disappointment to the family if you didn't."

Lorraine Abramson, who went to Morris High School in the

Bronx and City College of New York at the same time Powell did, remembered that Powell showed up in the Morris's Class of 1954 yearbook as the man who wanted to be an engineer. He lettered in track and was treasurer of the Service League, Abramson recalled. The Service League was a group that performed good deeds for the school.

"[Powell] was a friendly, always respectful gentleman," she said, but she admitted that at the time she never figured him as destined for national prominence.

"I was class valedictorian," she said, "but he's certainly turned out to be the most likely to succeed."

Although his early orientation was never focused on a career in teaching, Powell had been programmed by his parents to *believe* in education, and in spite of his antieducational bent throughout his youth, he knew he had to get himself a college education.

He had good enough grades to make it into college. The choice involved New York University or the City College of New York. NYU cost $750 a year; CCNY, $10 a year. From a practical standpoint of finances, he had *no* choice. He enrolled at CCNY.

His military bent surfaced there after a faltering start when he majored in geology. His early experiences with textbooks and teachers recurred. More or less to escape what he found to be drudgery, he enrolled in the Reserve Officers Training Corps—ROTC.

It was there that he came to realize he had a special ingrown talent he had never considered important. It was an intuitive sense of leadership.

He had a charismatic way with others, too, and his particular knack of being able to get other people to do what he wanted them to do surfaced dramatically in those years.

By the time he graduated at the top of his ROTC class in 1958—he never got anything above a C in any other classes— he was commander of the Pershing Rifles precision drill team and president of the Cadet Officers' Club. He graduated at the top of the ROTC class with the rank of cadet colonel, the top rank in the local ROTC.

"He was always in uniform," Abramson remembered. "He was actually very much like he is now."

Powell also belonged to House Plan, a kind of fraternity-type organization that "was one of the ways guys met girls."

However, throughout high school and college days, Abramson never remembered Powell going steady with anyone.

He has said that he chose ROTC for a career because black men in the fifties had few attractive opportunities on account of racism.

Powell once boiled down his success to what he called the thirteen rules he has always lived by.

Rule Number One: It ain't as bad as you think. It will look better in the morning.

Rule Number Two: Get mad, then get over it.

Rule Number Three: Avoid having your ego so close to your position that when your position falls, your ego goes with it.

Rule Number Four: It can be done!

Rule Number Five: Be careful what you choose. You might get it.

Rule Number Six: Don't let adverse facts stand in the way of a good decision.

Rule Number Seven: You can't make someone else's choices. You shouldn't let someone else make yours.

Rule Number Eight: Check small things.

Rule Number Nine: Share credit.

Rule Number Ten: Remain calm. Be kind.

Rule Number Eleven: Have a vision. Be demanding.

Rule Number Twelve: Don't take counsel of your fears or the fears of the nay sayers.

Rule Number Thirteen: Perpetual optimism is a force multiplier. (In the military, one is always looking for methods of increasing or multiplying one's forces.)

By the time he had graduated from CCNY, Powell had already selected his path in life. He would become a professional soldier. He knew he had found himself in his military role in college, and he felt he would be able to carry on as a soldier even after graduation.

Life for the military profession then had come on hard times, however. The Korean conflict had been settled when President Eisenhower had managed the cease-fire. There was little for a man in a military uniform to do but simply wait for action to come.

It would come faster than even Powell would guess. And it would come from a part of the world he had never even heard of.

3

Schwarzkopf:
Junior and Senior

Some fifty-odd miles southwest of Harlem and some light-years away in life-style lay Trenton, New Jersey, on the Pennsylvania border. It was there, three years before Colin L. Powell was born, that H. Norman Schwarzkopf saw the first light of day—on August 22, 1934.

His mother, Ruth, was a nurse, and his father, also called Norman, although that was not his first name, was a West Point graduate, class of 1917.

Technically, H. Norman Schwarzkopf was *not* a Junior, although he was named after his father—at least, to a visible degree. What was invisible was the fact that the "H" in the newborn baby's name was simply an initial that did not stand for anything at all. Like the "S" in Harry S. Truman, the "H" in Schwarzkopf's name was put there simply to make him the first male offspring of his father.

The father's first name was Herbert, but Schwarzkopf Senior was not enamored of the name, possibly because of the derogatory word association in the nineteen-thirties with the most derogative name in history—Herbert Hoover, the man many thought had brought on the Great Depression.

Young Schwarzkopf was born into a world that seemed always to be aswirl in controversy. At birth and during his first years of life, the controversy did not swirl about him, but about his father, Schwarzkopf Senior. And because young Schwarz-kopf always had an unalloyed admiration for his father, and because he modeled himself carefully after the image his father created, it might be well now to examine the similarities and differences between father and son. In fact, a study of the father himself—the son's roots—would certainly be in order to determine the son's particular attraction to the controversial and the contentious.

Schwarzkopf Senior was born in Newark, New Jersey, on August 28, 1895, the son of two immigrants from Germany. Schwarzkopf Senior's father was named Christian Schwarz-kopf, from the town of Pfedelbach in the Black Forest, Ger-many. There he was a miller, prior to his departure for the United States in 1855 at the age of twenty. *His* father before him ran a pub called the Rose in the tiny village of Sulz am Beckar before moving out and buying the mill his son ran.

Christian Schwarzkopf settled in Newark, New Jersey, and married another German immigrant, becoming a goldsmith in the country of his selection. Thus Schwarzkopf Senior grew up in a household that generally spoke German and had trouble making itself understood in English. But the American-born Schwarzkopf had no trouble with his schoolwork and turned out to be a very good scholar.

He was so good, in fact, that he won an appointment to West Point in 1913, and graduated number 88 in a class of 139. After graduating in 1917 from the Academy, the senior Schwarzkopf saw three months of active duty as an artillery officer in World War I, after which he was promoted to captain. With the war over so quickly after his arrival in France, he was faced with an important decision: should he continue his army career or get into some other line of business? With the "war to end all wars" now finished, it seemed to him that there might be little hope of making a good life for himself in the now discredited—by the public, at least—military service.

And so Schwarzkopf put out résumés for jobs in several different fields of endeavor. Meanwhile he stayed under the umbrella of army protection and served briefly in mustering out officers and men from the service. Actually, he had his eye on police work, and carefully studied several opportunities that offered themselves to him. The most ambitious of them was the challenge to create and maintain an organization of state police for the state of New Jersey.

When he was twenty-six years old, Schwarzkopf Senior was selected to inaugurate what became the New Jersey State Police. He was hired more for his proven abilities in military command than for professional instincts and training in police work. That is, he was far more military than civilian in his concept of the job.

This was to prove a factor in the major controversy into which he was thrust on the night of March 1, 1932—two years before the birth of his son. Then serving in the job as head of the state police in his third five-year term, Schwarzkopf was basking in the adulation of the citizens of New Jersey who thought that he had made a success of the quasi-military, somewhat elitist police organization he had created. The state police were prominent in the public eye with their campaign hats and smart horizon-blue uniforms with flaring yellow-striped riding breeches.

The adulation was premature, if not ill-considered.

It was on the night of March 1, 1932, that two New Jersey celebrities—Charles A. Lindbergh and Anne Morrow Lindbergh—discovered that their firstborn child, Charles A. Lindbergh, Jr., was missing from his nursery. Since the Lindberghs' residence, located in a remote part of New Jersey called Sourland Mountain, fell under state jurisdiction, Schwarzkopf, as commanding officer of the state police, took over the case, aided by his immediate deputies.

By now Schwarzkopf was a colonel, just as the kidnap victim, Charles Lindbergh, was. But Colonel Schwarzkopf was cognizant of the celebrity of the Lindberghs and tended to defer to Lindbergh's wishes.

A crudely made wooden ladder was found near the scene of the crime, along with a ransom note that immediately flagged the disappearance as a crime. The note was scrawled in broken English, with the obvious indication that the writer was of German extraction. "Good" was spelled "gut" [the child is in gut care].

Because of the extreme celebrity of the parents of the kidnapped baby, the case became an instant sensation. Unhappily, the ensuing machinations of kidnapper contact, the delivery of twenty thousand dollars in ransom money, and so on produced no sign of the missing twenty-month-old boy. On May 12, however, the body of the dead child was discovered in a shallow grave no more than two miles from the Lindbergh house, in an isolated portion of the woods.

At that point one of the maids in the home of the parents of Anne Morrow Lindbergh committed suicide when the police came to question her. Now the case was one of murder, and the money that had already been paid was written off.

The ins and outs of the Lindbergh kidnapping case are unimportant in this story of the Schwarzkopfs, but the result of the unsuccessful ransoming of the baby had a great deal to do with the hurricane of criticism that soon engulfed Schwarzkopf and his New Jersey State Police.

Although eventually it was the tracing of the marked bills in the ransom payoff that led police to Bruno Richard Hauptmann, who was convicted and executed for the kidnapping, it was the evidence of a member of the United States Forestry Service, Arthur Koehler, that proved the wood used in the kidnap ladder—and the tools used to shape it—could be linked directly to Hauptmann.

It was Schwarzkopf who brought Koehler into the case.

Nevertheless, by the time the case against Hauptmann was being tried in Flemington, New Jersey, the eyes of the world were focused on the tiny community. Three hundred reporters were on the job—some of them well-known writers and celebrities in their own right: Walter Winchell, Edna Ferber, Arthur Brisbane, Fannie Hurst, Damon Runyon, Kathleen Norris, Alexander Woollcott, Adela Rogers St. John. It became a three-ring circus.

Even the First Lady—Eleanor Roosevelt—felt called upon to sympathize with the man on trial, since she did not condone the death penalty.

The trial started on January 2, 1935, more than two and a half years after the crime was committed. New Jersey had a new governor. As a Republican and one of the few elected in the Roosevelt landslide of 1932, Governor Harold Hoffman had a natural desire to protect himself from the storm of criticism unleashed by Hauptmann's defense attorneys.

It was he who became the principal critic of Colonel Schwarzkopf and the New Jersey State Police. The investigation eventually became known as "the most bungled in police history"—at least, in the words of Governor Hoffmann.

The Lindbergh kidnapping continues to this day to surface in books, studies, and arguments against capital punishment. Current revisionist dogma tends to zero in on Colonel Schwarzkopf. "There's no doubt in my mind that Schwarzkopf was a major part of the frame-up of Richard Hauptmann," Anthony Scaduto said recently. His book *Scapegoat* appeared in 1976. The alleged frame-up, he believed, was organized by Schwarzkopf, whom he termed a "frame-artist" and a "sycophant" of Charles A. Lindbergh.

Lindbergh's star set in the late thirties when he publicly renounced the United States and moved to England to live. Later, when he offered his services in World War II to the government, President Roosevelt turned a deaf ear to the offer, since he felt that Lindbergh had betrayed his country by pointing out the superiority of Hitler's air force. (Lindbergh was right, but he never got his commission to fight.)

Later, in the late 1970s, there was a television movie that featured Anthony Hopkins as a very sympathetic, sad-eyed Hauptmann—a sob-sister film, done as a kind of soap opera saga.

In 1985, Ludovic Kennedy wrote a book titled *The Airman and the Carpenter: The Lindbergh Kidnapping and the Framing of Richard Hauptmann.* It purported to show how the state police, under Schwarzkopf, cut too many corners in bringing Hauptmann to justice.

"In Schwarzkopf's behalf, I will say that he truly believed Hauptmann was guilty," Kennedy said recently. "Never doubted it. And they were trying to do anything to get him convicted."

But other writers do not hold to the "frame-up" theory at all. George Waller, in *Kidnap: The Story of the Lindbergh Case*, concluded that the main evidence against Hauptmann—the wood for the kidnap ladder and the tools used to shape it—was definitely Hauptmann's and linked the ladder to him explicitly.

So did Edward D. Radin in his collection of true crimes, *12 Against Crime*, in which he based his account on a monograph written by Arthur Koehler of the Forestry Service.

But long before these books came out, New Jersey Governor Harold Hoffman brought the smoldering embers to a blaze when he wrote a chilling memo to Schwarzkopf:

"Had ordinary sound police methods been used following the commission of the crime, many doubts entertained today might have been eliminated."

Hoffman did not confine his attacks on Schwarzkopf to memos. He talked to at least five police officers and offered them job security if they would testify to the fact that Colonel Schwarzkopf had deliberately framed Hauptmann for the kidnapping.

Hoffman even put pressure on the police commission for Schwarzkopf's dismissal, but failed to get it. However, when the time for Schwarzkopf's reappointment came up, Hoffman passed him over for someone else.

And so, quite suddenly in 1936, Schwarzkopf was out of work for the first time in his life. In looking around for work, he soon found it—where he least expected it. In show business!

In the middle thirties the Hollywood gangster cycle was in full swing. The image of the Federal Bureau of Investigation had been polished over and over again, and was enjoying prime-time listening—on radio.

In July 1935, NBC Radio had produced a show called *G-Men*. The subject of the first broadcast was the life and death of John Dillinger. Other shows dramatized the crimes and captures of various criminals—featuring the day's "Most Wanted Men and Women," and so on.

Phillips H. Lord, an actor who had played the homey character of Seth Parker for a daytime soap opera for years, became interested in varying his repertoire a bit. Inspired by NBC's *G-Men*, Lord took a new concept of the same idea to CBS and talked them into trying out a series in competition.

It debuted on January 15, 1936. The technical effects of the opening were absolutely riveting. First there was heard the piercing blast of a police whistle. (Remember that this was radio and not television. The *ear* absorbed all, the eye nothing.) After the police whistle, the sound of feet running down the street came on. Then quick shots were fired. The sound of a window broken to effect entry was heard. A burglar alarm screamed in the night. Police sirens screeched. The rat-a-tat of machine-gun fire followed, with tire squeals, and glass breaking again. The opening was an immediate sensation.

After the sounds, the voice came on—the voice of authority and faceless command:

"Calling the police! Calling the G-Men! Calling all Americans to war on the underworld!"

Then, after a stunning silence, the voice continued:

"Gangbusters! With the cooperation of leading law enforcement officials of the United States, *Gangbusters* presents *facts* in the relentless war of the police on the underworld. . . . Authentic case histories that show the never-ending activity of the police in their work of protecting our citizens!"

After a scene-setting statement, there would be a conversation between the announcer and an actor portraying a particular lawman or police official who would be involved in the story that was to follow.

Phillips Lord played the announcer at first, and usually discussed with some "official" a certain case; after a few minutes of background exposition on the crime, the two would fade into the background, and the story itself would begin with the principals acting out their parts.

One especially good gimmick of the show was the so-called list of clues at the end. These "clues" were actually detailed descriptions of men or women wanted for crimes. A kind of "most wanted criminal," as on later shows.

Gangbusters created a brand-new format—which was particularly arresting in its initial opening sound effects. In fact, the phrase "to come on like gangbusters" originated at the time, meaning anything that starts out with a strong, virile, action-oriented beginning.

The show lasted from 1936 through 1955.

On March 20, 1952, it opened on television, with the same strong beginning and the essential format, but with sight now as well as sound. It alternated with *Dragnet*, a wildly successful cop show starring Jack Webb. The problem was that Webb couldn't come up with a new film each week; the *Gangbusters* film filled the spot.

At the end of 1952, the dual show achieved a fantastic rating of 42, virtually all the audience available in its time slot. In 1953 *Dragnet* went weekly, and *Gangbusters* was canceled.

It was shortly after *Gangbusters* began on radio that Colonel Schwarzkopf, released from his duties as superintendent of the New Jersey State Police, took over for Phillips H. Lord and became the announcer of the show.

Young Schwarzkopf grew up constantly being ribbed by his peers for his father's *Gangbusters* work, but managed to keep his temper and smile through it all. World War II broke out— the Japanese bombed Pearl Harbor—in 1941, when the boy was only seven years of age. His father was reactivated in the army, although, of course, he had lost all seniority because of his long stint in the New Jersey State Police and his radio activities. Nevertheless, instead of assuming command of troops, the elder Schwarzkopf was interviewed by General George C. Marshall about a special job in the Middle East.

And so it was that in 1942 Schwarzkopf Senior flew to Iran on the orders of General Marshall to help the country organize its first national police force, setting it up along the lines of the New Jersey State Police, which Schwarzkopf had brought into operation years before.

There was very good reason for this move. The supply routes for U.S. matériel ran straight through Iran to the Soviet Union—which at that time was allied with the United States. Schwarzkopf set up the police force and stayed on in Iran— the modern name for ancient Persia—through the war years, promoted to major general at the time of his work there.

Schwarzkopf Senior was so impressed by the people and the culture of Iran that he would write voluminous letters to his family in New Jersey. Schwarzkopf Junior was in turn so impressed by the information that he absorbed every detail and, in doing so, became fascinated by the mysterious and exotic Middle East.

His sister Sally was not quite so gung-ho about Iran. Every

THE NEW AMERICAN HEROES 31

time one of her father's huge letters would arrive at the house in Trenton, she would groan.

"Reading these letters is like doing homework!" she once said.

Young Norman felt quite differently.

There was a war on, of course, and all he could do about it was dream of the far-off place where his father was, and see it through the words his father wrote in his letters home. And he was able to imagine to himself that interesting, far-off land.

The war ended in 1945, and in 1946 Schwarzkopf Senior was able to wangle a trip for the entire family—his wife, Ruth, and the three children—to come to Teheran, the capital of Iran.

Young Schwarzkopf was twelve years old at the time. It was probably the most glorious adventure he had ever had. From the beginning he was fascinated with the Middle East, and that fascination would never fade.

Ironically, the Middle East was written into his future, as the Islamics might put it, but he did not know about that yet.

Schwarzkopf received an assignment to travel to Rome to establish a United States military advisory group. It was a postwar assignment, and occupied him for a year or two. He was then sent to West Germany to supervise the reorganization of the U.S. military police. He worked there until 1951, when he was rotated back to the United States.

By 1953 Schwarzkopf Senior found himself once again in the thick of the action—and in the midst of controversy. He was recalled to Teheran to act again as adviser to the Iranian National Police. Politically, Iran had been in a state of flux throughout the years during the war, and things were coming to a head in the struggle between the monarchy and the political parties that ran the country.

In 1941, on the eve of total war, the Shah of Iran, Reza Khan, formerly a military leader who had assumed the role of Shah in 1925, had abdicated, to be succeeded by his son, Mohammed Reza Pahlavi. The government in 1951 was in the hands of Premier Mohammed Mossadegh who decided to nationalize the country's oil resources. This move infuriated Great Britain, which had big and important holdings in Iranian oil. The British government immediately blockaded the Persian Gulf.

According to a memorandum written by C. M. Woodhouse of British intelligence, the idea was to get the Americans interested in helping depose Mossadegh—the real purpose being to save the Anglo-Iranian Oil Company (AIOC).

"The Americans," Woodhouse wrote in a memoir of the operation, "were more likely to work with us [the British] if they saw the problem as one of containing Communism rather than restoring the position of the AIOC."

Woodhouse, the story went, met with Kermit Roosevelt of the Central Intelligence Agency—recently formed in the United States out of the remnants of the Office of Strategic Services (OSS). The two of them met in Washington with Allen Dulles of the CIA. It was there that it was decided to replace Mossadegh with one of their own selections. He was a man named General Fazzlollah Zahedi, formerly head of the National Police.

There was a problem, according to Christopher Hitchens, who had written a book in which the overthrow of Mossadegh was studied. The problem was that Zahedi was a leading pro-Nazi in Iranian politics during World War II—so much so that he was kidnapped by the British and flown to internment in Palestine (now Israel).

In spite of any misgivings—it was sometimes difficult during World War II to tell the difference between the average Arab and a Nazi sympathizer—the British and the "cousins" decided on Zahedi anyway.

The CIA then approached Schwarzkopf as adviser to the National Police and asked for his help. And Schwarzkopf was put together with Zahedi to work out some method to try to wrest power from the hands of Mossadegh.

They succeeded—dramatically. What the two did was to arrange clandestinely for mobs of demonstrators to parade through Teheran, protesting the moves of the government, being careful not to tip their hands and show that they were working with the U.S. and Britain. With the "demonstrators" marching, the Shah on August 13, 1952, signed a decree removing Mossadegh as prime minister and nominating General

Zahedi as prime minister-designate. In the turmoil that followed, the Shah flew to Baghdad and then on to Rome. The planned anti-Mossadegh demonstrations occurred and the Zahedi supporters rallied. The government, somewhat shaky and never really solidly entrenched, fell, and Mossadegh was driven into exile.

The Shah—Mohammed Reza Pahlavi—was reestablished as head of the government on August 22. The CIA-British coup was so effective that it sewed up a great deal of Iran's oil output. According to Hitchens, AIOC, now known as British Petroleum (BP), was concessioned out, with Standard Oil of New Jersey, Standard Oil of California, Gulf Oil, Texas Oil, and Socony-Mobil, along with eight smaller U.S. Companies, awarded a percentage—raising the take from nil to 60 percent of all Iranian oil.

In the give-and-take of international "deals", the agreement spawned an arms, aid, and training program that made Iran the most powerful U.S. Gulf ally until the revolution in 1979, when the Shah was deposed.

"With the overthrow of Mossadegh," Hitchens wrote, "Schwarzkopf Sr. and his bosses thought their troubles were over. Even at the time, it was obvious to some that they were just beginning."

In his memoirs, Woodhouse said that if he had it all to do over again, he would not have trusted the Shah to govern his people wisely and kindly; nevertheless, in retrospect, Iran under the Shah seems to have functioned better than Iran under the Ayatollah Khomeini, who replaced him at the head of government in 1979.

"Stormin' Norman clearly is not genetically responsible for his father's role in helping to pick a Hitler fan to govern Iran," Christopher Hitchens wrote in *The Nation*, referring to Zahedi. Nevertheless, the implication remains that the controversy that swirled around his father might be about to swirl around him.

While the senior Schwarzkopf was living out his life as a top-grade officer in the army—he died on November 25, 1958—his son was just beginning to get his feet on the rungs of the ladder to follow in his father's footsteps.

The controversy that swirled around his father had not yet begun to swirl around him.

But it was just a matter of time before the storm would descend on him.

4

Schwarzkopf:
Target, West Point

While controversy swirled constantly around H. Norman Schwarzkopf Senior, the early life of H. Norman Schwarzkopf Junior was singularly placid and uneventful.

From the age of four, he knew what he wanted out of life. He wanted to be like his father, a West Point graduate and a field officer in the army.

Young Schwarzkopf grew up in a small town named Morrisville, a quiet suburb of Trenton, New Jersey. The burb was located not in New Jersey, but in Pennsylvania, just across the Delaware River from Trenton.

The town was steeped in military history. George Washington had made Morrisville his command headquarters in 1776, from December 8 to December 14. At that time it was a settlement of mansions on spacious estates—a quiet community of country gentlemen.

Not ten miles up the Delaware River, George Washington made his famous crossing of the Delaware on Christmas night, 1776. The house in which young Schwarzkopf grew up had been designated a historical landmark, as had many of the Morrisville homes.

The youth's days were spent in about the same pursuits that usually occupy the lives of growing boys in the United States. One of his boyhood friends, Ross Bevin, recently recalled:

"That's the guy I climbed trees with and played cops 'n' robbers and all that kind of stuff. We had a good time playing together. We were next-door neighbors."

Bevin recalled that young Schwarzkopf knew all about the historical ties his hometown had with the past—and reveled in it. He was, according to Bevin, "a guy who always wanted to wear a white hat."

Wearing a white hat in those days did not mean quite the same thing it came to mean later in America—in no way was there a hint of bigotry there. Once, when young Schwarzkopf was in a bus traveling from Lawrenceville to Princeton, he saw an elderly black woman standing in the aisle.

He rose and offered her his seat. She took it, and he stood.

The people seated around him chuckled and began kidding him. He was flustered and did not know how to respond. He had been taught differently from them, it was obvious, and he was confused.

When he arrived home, he questioned his mother about the incident, feeling that he had done something wrong, or at least something that had marked him as "different." Of course, he had always been aware that he was "privileged," not only because of his father's successful career in the army and in the state police, but also because the Schwarzkopfs were white. Was it not right, he asked his mother, to respond positively and helpfully to those of another color?

"Remember this," his mother told him sternly. "You were born white. You were born Protestant. You were born an American. Therefore, you're going to be spared prejudices other people will not be spared. But you should never forget one thing. You had absolutely nothing to do with the fact you were born that way. It was an accident of birth that spared you this prejudice."

Later, Schwarzkopf looked back on that episode with a smile. "I just grew up liking people," he said. "I tend to judge people on what kind of human beings they are, and I like to be judged the same way. I like people to look at the net worth of Norman Schwarzkopf, and I hope they judge me on what kind of heart I have in me."

A lot of that "heart," Schwarzkopf always knew, came from

his father, a man whom his son remembered always as a "compassionate guy, a very tough commander loved by his troops."

Young Schwarzkopf was only seven years old when the Japanese attacked Pearl Harbor and World War II got under way when the United States declared war on Japan—and later, on Germany. His father was called back into military service at the time and was away from home like all the other fathers were.

And it was Schwarzkopf Senior who was instrumental in plotting out the lines of education young Schwarzkopf would be following on his way to a military career, which both knew was exactly what young Schwarzkopf wanted.

The first step Schwarzkopf Senior took was in enrolling his son in Bordentown Military Institute near Trenton. It was an open secret in the Schwarzkopf home—now composed of young Schwarzkopf and his two sisters—that without a father's presence in the household, young Norman would be dominated by women, and possibly even overwhelmed by their ubiquitous presence.

That was the reason he was sent to military school—so he wouldn't "have to be home with three females"—in the words of his older sister, Sally.

He took his training at military school very seriously. When he was ten and a cadet at Bordentown Military Institute, the school ordered him to have pictures taken for the yearbook. It was now 1944, and war was raging all over the globe.

Young Norman was sent to the photographer, who dutifully took all the proper shots. Like any other photographer, he insisted on at least one gleaming, toothpaste smile—and young Schwarzkopf detested that.

The proofs came to the house, and his mother quite predictably selected the smiling picture over all the others for publication. However, young Schwarzkopf had other ideas. He argued long and stormily with her over the issue. He wanted the unsmiling, grim picture.

"Someday," he told her, "when I become a general, I want people to know that I'm serious."

Two years later, in 1946, the war was over and the country was trying to get back on its feet after its long period of international conflict and sacrifice on the home front. Young Schwarzkopf was twelve years old and anxious to continue with his military education.

It was at that time that Schwarzkopf Senior, still stationed in Teheran, Iran, managed to obtain trips to the Middle East for his entire family. The three children and their mother traveled to Teheran, where Major General Schwarzkopf was still acting as adviser to the National Police.

Young Schwarzkopf became steeped in the tradition of modern Persia. He had always been fascinated by the battles that took place there, including the Battle of Arbela in which Alexander the Great had wiped out a superior force of Persians under Darius—a force that included, according to some (probably inaccurate) historical estimates, a million men. In those days an army of a million men was a huge, unbelievable number, comparable to the percentage of the world's population involved in World War II.

But even more than the ancient battles that had been fought in the area, young Schwarzkopf became fascinated by the people who lived there, seemingly always living out their lives against a background of conflict and strife.

It was the youth's first exposure to the exotic ways of people who lived outside the United States of America. And he loved the life, exulting in the strange climate, in the people he met, and in the life-style of those people.

He never guessed, of course, that this experience would be a foreshadowing of probably the most exciting and successful moments of his future.

After his stay in Teheran, Schwarzkopf Junior was bundled off by himself to a year of study in Switzerland. There he began studying languages, specifically French and, later, German. His father was aware of the value of both languages to anyone who wanted to enroll at West Point. He also guessed that the postwar world would feature a great deal more internationalism than the prewar world had.

Thus, after a year in Switzerland, young Schwarzkopf was posted to Germany, where he continued his studies, now concentrating on German. Finally, after two years there, he was sent for a half year to Italy, where he finished up his language studies.

Once back in the United States, Schwarzkopf was enrolled at Valley Forge Military Academy where one of his teachers, Milton Medenbach, even at that time was impressed by the young man's aptitude.

"Good enough was never good enough for Norm," he said in a recent reminiscence. "It had to be *excellent*."

By now young Schwarzkopf was approaching the age of seventeen, and he knew he was facing a crucial test. Could he make it into West Point? The fact that his father had been there before him certainly did not hurt his chances at an appointment.

And, not surprisingly, he *was* accepted in 1952, and eagerly set out for the Academy. Even then he was thinking ahead to the future when he would be a full-fledged officer in the armed service—the dream he had had since he was a small boy.

Yet Schwarzkopf entered an institution that had been rocked to its foundations the year before by one of the most serious scandals in its history. West Point in 1951 had been forced to expel a number of cadets on the football team for violating the honor code. In effect, they had cheated on their exams.

This event had a significant effect on the young cadets who entered the school in 1952. Major David Horton, one of Schwarzkopf's roommates, said that this scandal had made a very real impact on all of the plebes.

"The honor system was very diligently instilled in all of us," he said. It was one influence, Horton pointed out, that helped produce in Schwarzkopf "a man of towering integrity."

Another friend of Schwarzkopf at the Academy agreed with Horton. "When [Schwarzkopf] says what is going on, it *is* what is going on."

From those first years as a plebe, young Schwarzkopf had to endure an especially grueling torment: the upper classmen thought it was hilariously amusing to haze this young man in an unmerciful manner. One of their favorite ploys was to force Schwarzkopf to mimic the sounds of sirens and burglar alarms and screeching tires and machine-gun fire and police whistles in order to mock his father's work on the old *Gangbusters* radio show.

The young man weathered it all in good spirits. He never minded—at least, not on the surface. What he *thought* remains censored in his own mind. His feelings would surface later in life when asked who his favorite model was: it was always his father he mentioned first.

Nevertheless, in spite of those rather unhappy beginnings at the Point, he excelled in soccer, football, tennis, and wrestling. For some odd reason, he never took to baseball. He was a big man now, getting his proper stature, build, and girth.

The Academy was not all hazing and study. Horton recalled sessions in which the roommates took turns reading aloud to each other. They read poetry, fiction, history. They went through *Huckleberry Finn* word for word. They would entertain each other with accounts of battles and imagine themselves in command of the troops.

One favorite bit of verse that emerged from these sessions, written by some unknown poet, went like this:

> *Here dead lie we because we did not choose*
> *To live and shame the land from which we sprung.*
> *Life, to be sure, is nothing much to lose;*
> *And young men think it is; we were young.*

Another of Schwarzkopf's roommates at West Point, retired General Leroy Suddath, remembered Schwarzkopf well. Suddath had always marveled at Schwarzkopf's "single-minded ambition."

"He saw himself as a successor to Alexander the Great, and we didn't laugh when he said it," Suddath recalled.

"Norm's favorite battle was Cannae," he explained, in which Hannibal crushed the forces of Rome in 216 B.C. "It was the first real war of annihilation, the kind Norman wanted to fight."

According to Suddath, Schwarzkopf was nurturing ambitions for the future, thinking about the time when he would be able to lead his country's forces in a major battle.

"We'd talk about these things in the wee hours," Suddath said, "and Norman would predict not only that he would lead a major American army into combat, but that it would be a battle decisive to the nation.''

Many years later Schwarzkopf took umbrage at Suddath for revealing to *Time* magazine that as a cadet, he had predicted he would be another ''Alexander the Great,'' leading armies to historic victories.

''I have never had any illusions to grandeur,'' he told a reporter in an attempt to lay to rest the ''Alexander'' role model. ''I will confess that sometimes the awesome responsibility that is placed on my shoulders flat scares me to death.''

Already in those formative years the mystique of H. Norman Schwarzkopf was forming. His IQ was reported to be 170— very far up in the genius category. Suddath thought he could easily have graduated first in his class of 480, but he did not.

''He did a lot of other things except study,'' Suddath said, mentioning wrestling and playing tennis, soccer, and football.

Schwarzkopf turned out to have an excellent tenor singing voice. What was more, he loved ballet music—an unusual thing in the macho atmosphere of West Point in those postwar years.

As a senior, he was selected to conduct the West Point choir. Later in his life, Schwarzkopf was to compare conducting music and leading troops with the following pithy assessment:

''In war the orchestra starts playing, and some son of a bitch climbs out of the orchestra pit with a bayonet and starts chasing you around the stage.''

The music that most appealed to Schwarzkopf was ''battle music''—the music composed by Pyotr Ilich Tchaikovsky to celebrate the great (at first *triumph*, but later) *defeat* of Napoleon at Waterloo—the *1812 Overture*. He also reveled in the martial music of Wagner, which he called ''uplifting.''

This music was, according to Suddath, ''the sort that makes you feel on top of the world.''

Many of his teachers at West Point remembered Schwarzkopf vividly. He was hard to ignore. Not only did he tower over his contemporaries in physical height, but he was their superior in many other ways, including intellect. Lieutenant General Harold Moore, for example, recalled him clearly.

''I was immediately struck by his leadership ability and

quick, alert mind,'' he said, ''and there aren't too many I remember from the hundreds I taught there.''

Steven Canby, a classmate who later became a teacher of military history at Georgetown University, remembered Schwarzkopf as ''brilliant, not flashy, but very smart. I know his staff says he was a 170 IQ, but I don't remember his playing it up.''

Lieutenant General Dave Palmer also recalled Schwarzkopf. ''I think it was pretty obvious at that point [that] he was a leader in the corps. He was the company commander of his company and people did tend to look up to him at that point.''

In his senior year, Schwarzkopf demonstrated once again his own interior mettle and his individuality. Most West Point seniors opted traditionally to sign up for the field artillery, which was the service the ''best and the brightest'' usually selected. Schwarzkopf, however, had always had it in mind to go in for the infantry, where his father had served.

Nor did Schwarzkopf let his decision to do so rest quietly in his own mind. He told everybody. In addition to getting the word around, he recruited friends to join him in the infantry. In effect, he led an underground campaign on the campus to recruit the so-called best and the brightest of the class of 1956 for the least glamorous but most important branch of the service.

He and his friends swarmed over the campus, mounting oversized replicas of the Combat Infantryman's Badge on trees and walls around the Academy. It was a reminder that the most respected decoration on any officer's chest would show that he served and led the Queen of Battle. The infantry.

These dissidents from the norm succeeded so well that Schwarzkopf's ''revolt'' led a large number of the class in the same direction he was traveling. As proof of his enormous clout, the elite artillery that year was forced to include among its members the Class Goat—the student ranked last academically among its senior cadets.

This move could hardly have pleased Schwarzkopf Senior. Schwarzkopf Junior once said:

''I think he thought I was never going to go anywhere; he was convinced the high-tech army was the place to be. If my dad were alive today, he'd be amazed that, as a mud-foot infantryman, I've gone from second lieutenant all the way to four-star general.''

''Norm aimed for the top and expected to reach it,'' his roommate Suddath said with a chuckle. ''I was concerned about how to be a good brigadier general. He was concerned about how to be a good four-star.''

In 1956 H. Norman Schwarzkopf was graduated from West Point, number 43 in a class of 480. He was officially a second lieutenant in the infantry division of the army.

5

Second Lieutenant Powell: Onward and Upward

Upon graduation from City College of New York in 1958, Colin L. Powell was commissioned a second lieutenant in the army. He was posted to several different army camps and spent his time as a junior officer getting used to the army way of life.

From the start, he flourished on it. In general, the life in the army at the time was relaxing and unfrantic. The Korean conflict had been neutralized, and America seemed far from any kind of war.

What he did not know—and what most Americans did not know—was that in one spot of the world things were cooking up into a low boil that would become a hot spot of war in a very few years. It was a tiny place called Vietnam.

There had been turmoil there for years. As far back as 1953, President Dwight D. Eisenhower had given France sixty million dollars to help it carry on what had become known as the "Indochina War."

One year later, unhappily, the French had surrendered to the Chinese communists at the fall of Dienbienphu. The Geneva Conference then divided Indochina into four parts: South Vietnam and North Vietnam; and Laos and Cambodia as independent countries in the west.

Now war broke out between North and South Vietnam, with

the Chinese communists helping North Vietnam and the U.S. pledging help to South Vietnam. In 1955 the United States agreed to help train the South Vietnamese army, but no men or arms were forthcoming for the moment.

By 1960 a full-fledged war was raging. Communist-led guerrillas aided by North Vietnam moved against the government of South Vietnam in a show of strength. South Vietnam proved to be a tottering regime that seemed doomed to defeat.

Ngo Dinh Diem, the premier of the government of South Vietnam, continued to request aid from the United States, which eventually was given. Under the leadership of President John F. Kennedy, special "military advisers" were sent to South Vietnam in order to bolster the sagging forces of the premier.

Soon 16,000 Americans were in South Vietnam working under the leadership of the South Vietnamese military. One of these advisers was Second Lieutenant Colin L. Powell.

During this period, Powell had been on a blind date in Boston one night when he met Alma Vivian Johnson, who had a master's degree in speech pathology and audiology. The two of them continued going together, and were married on August 25, 1962, just before Powell was to change posting once again.

Soon after they were married, he got the word that he would be going to Vietnam—one of President Kennedy's sixteen thousand advisers there. Their first child, Michael, was born while he was off in the jungles of South Vietnam working near the North Vietnamese border.

Two weeks passed before Powell even knew his son had been born.

Powell served in South Vietnam from 1962 to 1963, working with a South Vietnamese infantry battalion that patrolled the Laotian border. In 1963 Diem was assassinated, and the government was barely able to survive.

President Kennedy promised more help against the incursions of the North Vietnamese army. It was during this time that Powell inadvertently stepped into a Punji-stick trap, which lay concealed immediately below the surface of the water through which he was moving.

The stake impaled his left instep and came out the top of

his foot. In immense pain, he was shipped to Hue to have the wound treated. In spite of the wound, he returned in a matter of weeks to lead combat missions against the enemy.

He received a Purple Heart for his wound. That same year he also won a Bronze Star.

Returning to the States, Powell served routine duties in one post after another. A second child was born, this one a girl, named Linda. He would have three children, the third Annemarie.

Ironically enough, Powell learned about race prejudice not in Harlem at all, but in the Deep South. When he was still in Vietnam, his wife and baby daughter lived at her parents' home in Birmingham, Alabama, and, said Powell, "When Bull Connor and his damned dogs were running up and down the street . . . my father-in-law was guarding the house with a shotgun."

That summer in 1963, Powell said, "Police dogs, bombs, water cannons, mobs, and cattle prods were being used to suppress blacks who were determined to exercise their fundamental rights of assembly and access."

That same year Powell encountered racism firsthand. He was driving to his base through Sylacaugo, Alabama, "in a little German Volkswagen with New York license plates and an 'All the Way with LBJ' sticker on it."

As he sped through the city at seventy miles an hour, a state police car stopped him. The white cop who got out was handing out "Goldwater for President" stickers. Powell described the incident in this manner:

"He looked at me, the German car, the New York license plate, and the LBJ slogan. There was a moment of suspense. He finally said, 'Boy, get out of here. You are not smart enough to hang around.' "

Years later Powell remembered another situation in which he encountered racism down South—this time in Columbus, Georgia.

"I was trying to get a small house so that my family could join me, and I stopped at this joint. A nice young lady asked me if I was an African student. 'No.' 'A Puerto Rican?' 'No.' 'You're Negro?' 'That's right.' 'Well, I can't bring out a hamburger. You'll have to go to the back door.' "

Things had gotten better since that time, of course. "It's different now, but we still have a long way to go. We should be grateful for what the men and women have done before. We cannot let the torch drop."

The army in the fifties had more racism in it than in the nineties. "When I came along in 1958, I was able to capture all of what was done before by men in segregated units denied the opportunity to advance. They had the potential as I might have had."

In 1963 Powell was reassigned to Fort Benning, Georgia, and it was there that he decided to take advanced study at the Army Command and General Staff College at Fort Leavenworth, Kansas.

After a year or two of classes, he decided to go to graduate school. When he was interviewed by the officer in charge of the school, he was turned down.

"Your college record isn't good enough," he told Powell.

Powell conceded that the man in charge of the college was right, but that did not mean that Powell was incapable of carrying the burden of the work. He took a long, hard look at himself and at his seeming inability to do well with tests, and began a stiff self-reorganization exercise.

He worked hard, studied carefully, and at the end of his courses he graduated in his class number 2 of 1,244.

Instead of some plush assignment, Powell was sent back to Vietnam for a second tour of duty with the United States infantry. While he was languishing out in the hinterlands, the *Army Times* came out with a story about the year's graduating class from Army Command and General Staff College at Leavenworth. The article profiled the top five graduates, including Powell. When Powell's division commander read the story, he recognized the name, and blew his top.

"I've got the Number Two Leavenworth graduate in my division, and he's stuck in the boonies?" he snapped. "I want him on my staff."

And so it was there that Powell served as a battalion executive officer and division operations officer from 1968 to 1969.

In his second tour in Vietnam he was injured yet again. This time the accident occurred in a helicopter crash. After the plane settled down, he helped drag troops from the smoking chopper.

He came away with vivid memories of that chopper crash and how he escaped quickly to safety, only to return to the about-to-explode wreckage to pull to safety a man whose helmet had become impaled on the controls.

It was this last act that earned him the Soldier's Medal—one of the service's most prestigious.

Vietnam was probably the most depressing part of his army career. And it was so not because of his own actions, but because of the army's failure in Vietnam. Powell always hated being reminded of Vietnam. Even the thought of watching a movie about it unsettled him.

As late as 1990, he told a reporter: "I don't watch Vietnam movies because I don't like them, and I can't sit comfortably still for them."

However, he never had the nightmares about Vietnam that other soldiers had.

"I had no ghosts requiring exorcism," he said. "I went as a professional soldier. I served twice as a professional soldier. I didn't have anything like the trauma that an infantryman, the draftee private in the front lines for six months, had. I was an officer. Most Americans who went to Vietnam came out and went back to life without having ghosts to chase them. Some had difficulties. I feel for those who have had difficulties."

He returned to the States in 1969, and it was at that point in his career that he was able to make his dream of earning a master's degree in graduate school come true. He went to The George Washington University, and there earned a master's degree in business administration.

After that he was again posted here and there, serving out his time. By 1972 he had been promoted to major, and it was then that he got his first break—and it was *big* one. In fact, it was a plum of a political position.

He had the good fortune to be chosen as a White House Fellow—a much-sought-after internship that usually groomed middle managers for higher positions.

It was, of course, a turning point in his career. Before that appointment, there was nothing in his postings to indicate that he would end up in anything other than an army uniform. Now, the sky was the limit!

Powell never learned who it was who had put in the good word for him, but when a top army personnel man phoned him that wonderful day in 1972, he could hardly believe his good luck.

These were the words he would never forget:

"Colin, the Infantry Branch wants one of its people to become a White House Fellow. We want you to apply."

Powell was then working as an analyst in the Pentagon— one of a thousand faceless drones. The good news was that once he had received that call and was instructed to apply, the matter to all intents and purposes was strictly pro forma. He was in.

Somehow, Powell had caught the attention of somebody important in the army. Whoever this somebody was had a great deal of clout—enough to arrange for Powell this "dream job," as Powell always thought of it.

His big break never went sour, as some big breaks do. Quite soon he was on intimate career terms with Caspar Weinberger, then director of the Office of Management and Budget, and with Frank Carlucci, Weinberger's deputy. These would be the two men who would help elevate Powell higher and higher in the Washington military hierarchy.

Actually, the "dream job" lasted but a year. It ended suddenly when an outside occurrence called for Powell's particular expertise, skill at command, and understanding.

In September 1973, a race riot broke out in the 1st Battalion, 32nd Infantry, which at the time was stationed in South Korea. It was a serious matter, and someone had to cool it.

Powell was the right man in the right job at the right time. When he arrived on the scene of the riots, he was appalled at the shambles to which the army had been reduced. The hatred was genuine, the hostility naked, and the animosity almost thick enough to be cut with a knife.

Mostly the problem had to do with boredom. With no war to fight, the troops were simply held there in suspension, to do what they liked. The obvious parallel was life in prison, only without the presence of dangerous people to threaten you. With boredom, of course, came drug abuse.

The battalion was riddled with addicts. And it was the drugs that helped provoke racial hatred between factions of white and black. Discipline had gone down the drain. There was no pride, no sense of dignity, no idea of responsibility—none of the elements that the army existed on.

It was no easy task to get things back to normal. Typically, Powell simply went by the numbers and proceeded to instill in the unit an old-fashioned supply of discipline and military exercise.

He isolated the ringleaders, investigated them, and threw the hard-liners, who had no business in the army anyway, in the brig. Then he drew up work charts and instituted roll calls, formations, drills, marching exercises—in fact, the works. In short, he put the troops to work when, actually, there was really no work to do.

He later said: "[We] threw the bums out of the army and put the drug users in jail. The rest we ran four miles every morning, and by night they were too tired to get into any trouble."

In no way was it quite that simple, but Powell was never a braggart or a loudmouth. His patience, his understanding, his steady, determined manner were the elements that helped solve the problem.

Some months later he was able to return to the States, having fulfilled his mission. Blacks and whites were not only working together harmoniously, they were socializing after work as well.

It was in 1974 that Powell, now a full colonel, returned to the States to take a staff job in the Pentagon. He stayed there for a year and then enrolled in the National War College. Having completed only seven of the nine arranged courses of study, he was surprised to receive, quite unexpectedly, command of the Second Brigade of the 101st Airborne Division at Fort Campbell, Kentucky.

Even without attending the last two months of study, he graduated the course with distinction. This was quite a different story now from the saga of his Harlem school days!

He served at the 101st Airborne Division for two years, then was transferred back to Washington. He was given the position of senior military assistant to the Deputy Defense Secretary in the administration of Jimmy Carter, and, in 1979, he moved on to the job of executive assistant to the Secretary of Energy Charles W. Duncan, Jr. Powell had attained by now the rank of major general.

The spring of 1981 found Powell starting in on a two-year assignment as assistant commander of the 4th Infantry Division at Fort Carson, Colorado.

While serving as deputy commander at Fort Leavenworth, Kansas, in July 1983, Powell was called back to Washington by Caspar Weinberger, now Secretary of Defense for President Ronald Reagan. Powell then became Weinberger's senior military assistant, and stayed in the job for three years.

In this important position, Powell was *the* ne plus ultra as Weinberger's segundo. He winnowed the chaff from the wheat when it came to visitors and information that went to Weinberger's office.

It was also in this position that he showed his flair for getting along with virtually everybody. He also earned the reputation for being cool, politically astute, and having a sense of humor. The story that describes Powell to a T was the one about his waking up one day in 1983, only to hear to his dismay that the Defense Department intended to start shooting dogs for medical experiments in a military laboratory. He later discovered to his horror that these dogs were beagles.

Powell sensed a public-relations disaster if these experiments were allowed to proceed as scheduled. Quickly, Powell briefed Weinberger about the experiments and concluded:

"Shooting Snoopy just isn't going to work!"

Weinberger saw the point and Powell ordered the Defense Department to halt the experiments.

Powell's aide-de-camp at the time, Captain James Cormack of the navy, said of Powell: "He didn't even want to find out whether the dog-shooting program was right, wrong, or indifferent. He's a realist, and this just wasn't going to fly."

When America sent forces to invade the island of Grenada in the British West Indies in 1983, Powell forestalled the White

House and National Security Council staffs from interfering with the military while concomitantly keeping them filled in on the invasion's progress.

One associate said proudly of Powell: "He won't bother the boss with third-rate details, but will make sure that the first-rate details get the right attention."

His cool personality, which never appeared to get rattled under the gun, seemed always able to put others at ease, and according to one admirer, Powell had "an uncanny ability to defuse tense situations."

During the Grenada invasion, his exact assignment, coming directly from his boss, Weinberger, was to "keep the White House and the National Security Council staff out of the detailed planning, informed but off the back of the military. He did it, and managed not to ruffle any feathers."

After his stint with Weinberger, which lasted from 1983 to 1986, Powell was assigned to the United States V Corps in Europe. A year later he became the Deputy National Security Adviser for President Reagan, and in short order became the National Security Adviser in 1987 on Carlucci's resignation.

In 1988 he was Commander of the Armed Forces Command, only to be selected by President Bush in 1989 to be the Chairman of the Joint Chiefs of Staff.

Powell once said that he never saw a WASP until he was stationed at Fort Benning.

"I was stationed in Fort Benning before I ever saw what is referred to as a White Anglo-Saxon Protestant."

And it was back in 1964 that he encountered racism in short order when he and his wife, Alma, were refused service at Buck's Barbecue, a restaurant in Columbus, Georgia. Bartenders all over that city refused to serve Powell.

Oh, the racism was real, all right.

Jesse Jackson never believed that Powell was committed enough to the cause of civil rights. "When we needed the Voting Rights Act extended, where was the voice of George Bush and his party?"

Later on, when there was some talk about Powell running as Republican Vice President, Jackson told *The Washington Post*: "It would change the political equation in this country by as much as the vote shift from blacks voting Republican and blacks voting Democratic under Roosevelt in 1932.''

In a vicious backhand compliment, Jackson added that Powell was an ''able national security chief who has somehow been a rose that emitted fragrance in the middle of a sleazy pond. Somehow that stench has not touched him.''

He concluded by saying, ''Will [Powell] be put on the market is the question, and the answer is not likely.''

Powell declined to serve as grand marshal for a parade honoring Martin Luther King, Jr., even though King was Powell's hero. The problem stemmed from the questioning by certain civil rights leaders of the selection of Powell for the honor.

Powell wrote a letter to Coretta Scott King, King's widow, noting that his presence might detract from the parade. He said he had to stay in Washington anyway.

Civil rights leaders had complained that Powell's presence at the parade would be an embarrassment at the Martin Luther King, Jr., Center for Nonviolent Social Change. Mrs. King said she was opposed to U.S. military involvement in the Persian Gulf and quickly accepted Powell's decision to withdraw from the parade.

Powell's son, Michael, grew up to become a first lieutenant in the United States Army. However, he had to leave the army with 100 percent disability after an all-but-fatal car accident in Germany, where he was serving. He then enrolled in a law course at Georgetown University.

Linda became a student of acting in New York City. Her first stage appearance occurred when she played the role of Rachel Robinson, the wife of the late baseball immortal, Jackie Robinson, in *Play to Win*, a musical comedy based on Robinson's life. It played at the Promenade Theatre in New York and then went on national tour.

''I am delighted at getting the part,'' Linda told a reporter for *Jet* magazine, ''particularly since it was my first musical audition.''

On the strength of her performance, she was tested and assigned a role in the motion picture *Reversal of Fortune*, in which she played one of the law students who helped Alan Dershowitz win Claus von Bulow's case. Then in 1991 she played a flirt in a small German town in the play *Judgment Day* at the Samuel Beckett Theater in New York.

When a reporter jokingly asked her about the possibility of her father's becoming President of the United States, she quipped back: "President? I hope I become famous first." She said that her father never did talk much about his work in Washington. "He guards his privacy," she said, "and his opinions. We're allowed to have our opinions and he has his."

About the Persian Gulf War, which had just been successfully concluded at the time of the interview, she said: "I'm glad it's over. I think we did what we had to do."

Colin Powell's younger daughter, Annemarie, is a freshman at the College of William and Mary in Williamsburg, Virginia.

6

Second Lieutenant
Schwarzkopf:
Vietnam

To backtrack to the military career of Second Lieutenant H. Norman Schwarzkopf just after his graduation from West Point in 1956, things did not look particularly bright for a man who had concentrated all his resources on becoming an officer in the army. In much the same manner as his father before him had faced a drought in good assignments after his war was over, young Schwarzkopf looked about him and saw that peace had broken out all over the world—theoretically.

The 1953 signing of the armistice in Korea had been the final nail in the coffin of worldwide war, yet trouble spots continued to flare up sporadically. If any time could be considered "better than ordinary" for a newly commissioned officer graduating from West Point, this was certainly not the "right" time.

His career, up to now viable and portending a dramatic and successful future, was definitely on hold. As a second lieutenant in the infantry, he was doomed to follow the familiar pattern of thousands of other peacetime graduates before him.

He was sent to Fort Benning, Georgia, where he was assigned to the infantry school there. As a fresh young officer, he went through the familiar courses in instruction and in command. For this young man with dreams of glory, it was not the most rewarding time in his life.

Soon he finished infantry school and was transferred to air-borne school, also at Fort Benning. There he learned the tactics of delivering troops onto fields of battle from the sky. The tactics of war were changing rapidly now, given the impetus of World War II and the brief action in Korea.

Command of the air had become more important than ever; but Schwarzkopf continued to believe in the necessity of ground war, since, of course, he was in the infantry, and had opted for that division of the armed services.

But he was bored. Worse that that, the personalities about him were not conducive to good social relations.

"I had an alcoholic commander," he said. "I had an executive officer who was a coward. I saw terrible things going on around me and I said, 'Who needs it? When my three years are up, I'm getting out!' "

Nevertheless, he did not get out. As Schwarzkopf later put it, "a very sage guy" got to him and told him to bear with it for a while.

"Young man," the sage guy said, "you know, if all the guys who see these bad things happening quit, then all the guys who don't think these things are so bad are going to be doing them later on. If you really think it's that bad, why don't you stick around until someday you get into a position to do something about it?"

Schwarzkopf saw the wisdom of this argument and surrendered to it. He thrust his chin out, took a deep breath, and held his tongue—for a while.

The army had just formed a new Strategic Army Corps (STRAC) division at Fort Campbell, Kentucky. After his two years of training and service at Fort Benning, Schwarzkopf was posted to Fort Campbell, where he continued his study and his training.

Although the work was routine and the life-style monotonous almost to the death, Schwarzkopf stuck to it. After all, what else was he really interested in as a career but the army? Soon enough he learned to cover up his boredom and his hostility toward the things he saw around him that he did not like. In short, he soldiered.

The postings continued in their undramatic fashion. After STRAC training, he was posted to Berlin, Germany, for two years, in command of bored, boring occupation troops who were then facing some formidable opposition from the Soviets—all of it sub rosa and unpublicized, but very real nevertheless.

The Cold War had begun to heat up. Berlin was the focal point of the Soviet action. The city would be split by the Berlin Wall in 1961—a high guarded wall that would remain in place until pulled down by physical force in 1989.

While in Berlin, of course, Schwarzkopf did all he could to polish up his German—the study of which had been his father's idea during his teen years. However, in the end the Berlin assignment proved to be a routine one, and he was posted back to the States, to Benning, once again to pursue his military studies.

This time he learned what it meant to be a "career officer," taking what was generally considered the course of that name. As he sat in classrooms and served the usual chores of the officer corps with the enlisted men, the Cold War assumed a much more intense heat in the outside world.

By the time the Cuban missile crisis erupted in 1962, no one really knew but what the entire armed services might not soon be on a marching basis. But it did not happen.

In 1963 Schwarzkopf opted for a course at the University of Southern California, there earning a master's degree in mechanical and aerospace engineering. To put this selection of study in its proper context, it was February 1962 that John Glenn had become the first American to orbit the earth in space. The American presence in space was a solid objective now, and the race with Russia well in place.

In two years he had his master's and was returned to West Point to begin a three-year teaching assignment. He did not particularly relish teaching; he wanted action. But there was not much he could do about it at that time, since his superiors wanted him on the teaching podium.

What was particularly eating at Schwarzkopf then was the

fact that several of his very best friends from the Academy had already died in the Vietnam conflict, which was just beginning to escalate. Among the 16,000 military advisers sent to Vietnam, several officers he had known had been killed.

He mourned their deaths, and he began agitating for assignment to Vietnam. He wanted not to avenge their deaths especially, but to prove to himself that he was what he had always hoped to be: a man who could shine in action.

He did not serve out his three consecutive years of teaching. Instead, he was posted to Vietnam in 1965. That February, eight American advisers were killed in their compound at Pleiku. Later, twenty-three more Americans died in an attack on their barracks at Qui Nhon. Things were getting more and more serious.

These deaths prompted President Lyndon B. Johnson to initiate Operation Rolling Thunder, which would sustain air bombardment of North Vietnam. One month later, in March, U.S. marines landed at Danang. By this time there were at least 27,000 troops in Vietnam. Two months later there were 46,000, and in June, 75,000. The buildup was under way.

Schwarzkopf arrived early in the summer and was immediately assigned to the Vietnamese Airborne Division. He was a qualified expert in the command of airborne troops and was made task force adviser. As a captain—he had been promoted recently to that rank—Schwarzkopf was instantly in the thick of battle.

The kind of war being fought in Vietnam involved the swift movement of troops over large areas of ground, and the only feasible way to move troops over large areas of impenetrable terrain and swamp water was by air.

Shortly after his arrival in the field, he spent ten days surrounded by the enemy at the Dak To Special Forces Camp. It was about a month afterward that Captain Schwarzkopf was promoted to Major Schwarzkopf.

"We fought almost every day of every month for thirteen months," Schwarzkopf said.

According to C. D. B. Bryan, an author who had long talks with Schwarzkopf after he had served two tours in Vietnam, "Schwarzkopf was proud of his unit, and of his own service."

He was always with the troops. "When they slept on the ground, I slept on the ground. What they ate, I ate. It was truly serving a cause I believed in."

Schwarzkopf summed up his first tour of duty in Vietnam this way: "I really thought we had done something good, just like George Washington. I had gone and fought for Freedom."

During those months, President Johnson authorized an escalation of U.S. forces in Vietnam from 75,000 to 125,000 men. That was in July 1965.

In 1966, Major Schwarzkopf was sent back to West Point to serve out his remaining two years of teaching as an associate professor in the Department of Engineering Mechanics. He flew almost nonstop from Vietnam to New York to get home.

"I was this soldier coming home from war," he recalled later. He thought there would be people there to greet him—but there were none. In fact, the terminal was empty.

He walked out into the fog that shrouded the city and got into a helicopter bound for Newark. After debarking from the helicopter and walking out into the street, he hailed a cab and gave the driver the address of his mother's home in East Orange. His father had died in 1958.

He might have expected the cabbie to notice his uniform and comment on it with a cheery "Just back from Vietnam?"

The cabbie said nothing.

Major Schwarzkopf said it himself. "Sure is great to be back in the U.S. again!"

Zilch. The driver didn't even seem interested in where Schwarzkopf had been.

It was the major's first realization that the Vietnam War was not playing well on the home front. He had been away too long to know what was happening.

He soon found out that the war in Vietnam was not accepted at all by the American public. For some reason it was seen as a "bad" war—as opposed to a "just" war.

Somewhat put down, Major Schwarzkopf returned to West Point to teach engineering mechanics for the two years left of his three-year assignment. It was during this rather slack and lackluster period of his life that he attended a football game one Saturday afternoon at the Academy and met a young woman named Brenda Holsinger, who was working as a flight attendant for TWA. She was twenty-six years old. Schwarzkopf began dating her.

In August 1968 Major Schwarzkopf was promoted to lieutenant colonel—far ahead of the majority of his contemporaries.

A short time later he and Brenda Holsinger were married at a ceremony held at West Point. At the age of thirty-four, Lieutenant Colonel H. Norman Schwarzkopf was posted to the Command and General Staff College.

Certainly for this young officer it was a great coup. His natural talent for command and his excellent record in Vietnam had obviously served him well and passed him far ahead of most of his peers.

By March 1969, the U.S. military forces in Vietnam reached their peak strength, with 541,000 men. Ironically enough, this number foreshadowed the number of combat troops that would be used in Operation Desert Storm in the Persian Gulf War in 1991.

In December 1969, Lieutenant Colonel Schwarzkopf was posted to Vietnam for a second tour of duty. There he assumed command of the 1st Battalion, 6th Infantry, 198th Infantry Brigade of the American Division.

On February 19, 1970, Michael Eugene Mullen, a member of Charlie Company, 1st Battalion, was killed in combat, apparently from a mortar shell lobbed by the command itself. In military parlance, Michael Mullen was killed by "friendly fire"—that is, fire delivered by South Vietnam and not by the enemy, North Vietnam.

Of all the casualties that would be absorbed by Schwarzkopf's battalion, this one would embroil him in the most controversy. At the time the incident occurred, he had no idea of what lay ahead of him.

On May 28, 1970, a little more than three months after the death of Michael Mullen, Schwarzkopf had his own turn of bad luck.

A number of men from Bravo Company, 1st Battalion, had been patrolling the forward area and had detonated a mine in a field. The company commander, who was a captain, and the platoon leader, a lieutenant, received bad wounds. The rest of the men were frozen in the field, afraid to move in any direction.

Immediately Schwarzkopf and his artillery liaison officer, Captain Bob Trabbert, called for a command helicopter and flew to the area. The two wounded men were immediately flown back by the chopper.

Schwarzkopf remained behind with Trabbert to get the patrol out of the mined field. Schwarzkopf knew exactly what had happened. The men simply did not know what to do. Their commanding officer had been injured; he was gone. So was their platoon leader. They felt trapped and—worse than that—abandoned by their superiors.

It was up to Schwarzkopf to get them out. He began to talk to them, trying to exorcise their fear. In as calm a voice as he could muster, he told them that they were going to be all right. He instructed them to walk out of the field the same way they had walked in.

His tone and attitude finally began to work on the patrol. Some of the men began to listen and heed his orders. Schwarzkopf continued talking steadily, knowing that calm would wear down their fear.

"Watch where you put your feet," he told them. "Keep to your old tracks. Stay calm. Keep your distance." It became a litany of words—dull, flat, but successful.

And then—

A young private about a dozen yards from Schwarzkopf stepped on another mine. He went up in the air and fell awkwardly on his side. Schwarzkopf and Trabbert were so close that they too were injured slightly.

Then Schwarzkopf saw the young soldier's right leg—it was flung out to one side and looked bad. At about the same moment, the soldier saw it too. He was in panic.

"My leg! My leg!" he called out, his voice rising into a scream.

A quick glance over the field told Schwarzkopf that the men were beginning to panic again.

"Keep still!" Schwarzkopf called out in a steadying voice. "Stay where you are!"

Somebody yelled for a medic. Schwarzkopf's voice cut across the turmoil and ordered Trabbert to radio the med-evac helicopter to hurry in for another victim.

"Keep still!" Schwarzkopf again told the patrol.

The wounded soldier was thrashing about. "Somebody help me, help me!"

Schwarzkopf began making his way slowly across the mined ground. Methodically. Carefully. Each step a prayer. "Don't move!" he cautioned the injured man as he continued forward. He had almost closed the distance between them when the soldier lost his head again.

"I'm going to die! We're all going to die!"

And then, to his own disbelief and incredulity, Schwarzkopf felt his legs begin to shake uncontrollably. He had never had the experience before; fear had taken complete control of him. His legs were stalks of vegetables. Sweat poured down off his forehead into his eyes.

What made it worse, he could see that every eye around him was focused directly on him. What was the matter with him? Why wasn't he continuing across the field?

Years later Barbara Walters asked Schwarzkopf if he was ever scared. The question was asked in such a way that the answer was obvious: never!

Schwarzkopf got a little grin on his face and his eyes brightened. "I've been scared in every war I've ever been in!" he told her, bluff and outspoken. But what he didn't tell her at that time was that fright never *stopped* him from doing what he had to do.

"I'll get you out," Schwarzkopf called across to the wounded soldier. "Keep still. You're all right."

"I'm not all right! Can't you see my leg?"

But Schwarzkopf had regained his self-command. He would tell C. D. B. Bryan where he had found that self-control. He suddenly thought of the sign Harry S. Truman kept on his White House desk: "The buck stops here." By transference, in war the buck stopped with H. Norman Schwarzkopf.

"Your leg is only broken," he told the soldier calmly. "I can tell that from here." Schwarzkopf could see the pieces of bone sticking out, and he warned him again not to move but to remain still.

Then the agonizing moments were over. He was there, lowering his body across the wounded soldier's body to keep him still.

"Don't you move around. We're going to have to set that leg."

Schwarzkopf glanced around to see what he could use for a splint, and saw that three of the men had regained the safety of the ground and were standing with Trabbert.

"God, it hurts, sir!" moaned the soldier.

Then Schwarzkopf saw the small, waist-high tree near the cleared ground.

"I'll need a splint for this man's leg," he told Trabbert. "One of you cut me some splints off that tree."

Trabbert handed his sheath knife to one of the men, who moved toward the tree. One step was enough. Another mine went off right under him.

"Oh, my God!" cried Schwarzkopf, horrified. Trabbert had taken the full force of the explosion. His left leg had been blown off, one arm broken backward, and a hole gouged in his head. He would survive.

The other three men with him were killed instantly. They lay where they had fallen, no one moving.

The young private pinned beneath Schwarzkopf twisted about to get a better view.

"Are they all dead, sir?"

For having crossed the mine field to rescue the wounded private, Schwarzkopf was awarded his third Silver Star.

According to Schwarzkopf, he had no other choice but to do what he did. It was his responsibility. By being there with the wounded man instead of standing back with Trabbert, he had inadvertently saved his own life.

"You live with these things," Schwarzkopf said. "You become terribly fatalistic in combat."

By the time it came his turn to go back to the States, Schwarzkopf could look back on two tours of duty in Vietnam with some manner of satisfaction. He had done his job. On his first tour he had served as a paratrooper advising Vietnamese airborne troops, and on his second he had served not only as a staff officer at U.S. Army Vietnam (USARV) but as a commander of an infantry battalion.

"I hated it in the rear," he said. "It was a cesspool. I went out to my battalion and I never went back to the rear except when ordered, maybe one time, to division headquarters. There you saw the worst; the commander was living in luxury, his focus was on things like the reenlistment rate. When I took over my battalion, it was totally unprepared for battle, yet it had been in battle. All they were doing was taking casualties, [not] inflicting them. It was a nightmare."

At the same time, he had done what he was assigned to do, and had also performed feats that were quite out of the ordinary. On one occasion, he had refused to take his Vietnamese unit into battle because commanders had forgotten to order adequate air and artillery support.

Schwarzkopf recounted another episode later. "The first time I ever lost my temper was in a situation at Duc Co [during my first Vietnam tour]. I had wounded Vietnamese lying on the ground who desperately needed air evacuation, and I had helicopters flying all over the place with VIPs in them, and I couldn't get the helicopters on the ground to get the wounded out of there.

"I can still remember it to this day, because I was yelling profanities over the airwaves. I can remember subsequently getting back to the States and suddenly I would lose my temper. How shocked I was, because it had never happened before."

Twice he had been wounded in action. When he was assigned as a staff officer to U.S. headquarters in the rear, he discovered that most of his peers in the officer corps seemed more bent on promoting their careers than on winning the war.

He had learned that there was less romance in war than despair and loss of hope.

"All you have to do is hold your first soldier who is dying in your arms and have that terribly futile feeling that 'I can't do anything about it, that the life is literally flowing out of this young man, and I can't do anything about it,' " he told one reporter in Vietnam just before returning home for the last time. "Then you understand the horror of war. Any soldier worth his salt should be antiwar."

His sister Sally had the final word on her brother's Vietnam experience.

"My brother as a young man was carefree and witty and charming," she said. "He went over to Vietnam as a heroic captain and came home very serious. He lost his youth in Vietnam."

By the time his second tour of duty in Vietnam was history, Lieutenant Colonel Schwarzkopf had won the following decorations:

The Combat Infantryman's Badge
The Command Parachutist Medal
Three Silver Stars
The Legion of Merit
The Distinguished Flying Cross
Three Bronze Stars (one with "V"["V" for valor])
Nine Air Medals
Four Army Commendation Ribbons (one with "V")
Two Purple Hearts
The Vietnamese Gallantry Cross
    (with two palms and two gold stars)
The Vietnamese Service Medal
The German Occupation Ribbon
The National Defense Medal

7

Lieutenant Colonel
Schwarzkopf:
Vietnam Redivivus

If Lieutenant Colonel H. Norman Schwarzkopf thought his
second return from the Vietnam war zone was going to be any
different from his first, he was mistaken. Or at least, he was
taken by surprise at the *increased* hostility he encountered on
his second return. His first had been greeted with apathy; now
there was real animosity expressed toward him.

"Not only was I *not* getting greeted and flowers thrown on
me and loved—except for Brenda, who was happy to see me—
this time when I came back, the uniform was spit upon and
people were calling me a baby burner."

Barbara Walters was interested in this statement, and questioned Schwarzkopf later: "You said people spit at you?"

Schwarzkopf's eyes glittered and he smiled crookedly at
that. "Oh, no!" he said softly but firmly. "Nobody ever spit
at me, and I can assure you, there would have been an immediate reckoning. But they spit at a lot of people in military
uniform."

She acknowledged the difference between spitting on "the
uniform" and spitting at "Schwarzkopf."

"Nobody," continued Schwarzkopf, repeating the word,
"nobody was going to spit at me. *Nobody!*"

Now he was beginning to sound like the Midas Muffler commercial.

She cut in: "After Vietnam, did you ever think of resigning from the army?"

"Oh, yeah. Sure. I thought about resigning from the army before Vietnam a lot of times, too."

"Why didn't you quit after Vietnam?"

"There were a lot of things that needed to be fixed, and if you quit and run away from it, then, you know, you're— you're. . . . That's not the time to quit, not when everything's broken. The time to quit is when everything's fixed!"

In the period of post-Vietnam, Schwarzkopf began giving speeches before civic organizations to get the real Vietnam story out. When he would finish, people listening to him would raise their hands and say things like:

"What about the babies you napalmed? What about the villages you burned?"

Schwarzkopf felt that television was doing a disservice to the American people. The broadcast medium seemed to be quite consistently depicting the career military officer as something of a horrible "Neanderthal," as Schwarzkopf expressed it. "A Neanderthal who with blind, unquestioning obedience burned villages and killed babies. And what made it so difficult [for me] was the fact that *I hadn't done any of that!*"

In the meantime, a nonbattlefield showdown that Schwarzkopf was quite unaware of was beginning to take shape. And when that confrontation occurred, the controversy it stirred was oddly reminiscent of the controversy that had swirled around Colonel H. Norman Schwarzkopf Senior of the New Jersey State Police in his day.

To put it briefly, the parents of the enlisted man named Michael Eugene Mullen became angered over the fact that their only son and other soldiers had died by "friendly fire" and because of that were not listed as casualties of the war. The Mullens turned against the war, using Michael's death benefit to pay for an advertisement in the *Des Moines Register*; soon a researcher found that, indeed, almost one-fifth of the Iowa deaths in Vietnam were not included in the Pentagon's casualty count.

Then a *New Yorker* writer, C. D. B. Bryan, was drawn into the controversy and assigned to explore the charges of the Mullens. The result of his interviews and his investigation into the tragedy resulted in the book *Friendly Fire*, which first appeared in serial form in *The New Yorker* magazine and was made into a motion picture later.

Had it not been for the emotionalism spawned by the war in Vietnam—blamed by some on the negative aspects played up and exploited by the news media (particularly television)—it is doubtful that the charges directed at Schwarzkopf would ever have been noticed at all.

But it was a strange war. The draft that had to be instituted to provide new recruits was unpopular with the public. Thousands of men of integrity deserted their country to live in Canada or Sweden. Some nights the news contained atrocities blamed not on the enemy, but on American troops.

In this kind of emotional climate, the charges against Schwarzkopf could not be ignored. In fact, they were picked up by other newspapers and magazines. When C. D. B. Bryan entered the fray, the Mullens had finally zeroed in on Schwarzkopf and were questioning him while he lay in bed recuperating from a wound.

The story that finally came out was one of numerous, continuous misunderstandings. The original letters purportedly from Schwarzkopf about the death of Michael Mullen had not been written by Schwarzkopf at all, but by someone else in the command. The investigation into the death of Michael Mullen, which the Mullens thought had been conducted by Schwarzkopf and which they termed a kind of whitewash, although that was not the word used, was actually conducted by someone other than Schwarzkopf.

And there were other differences between the opposing parties on both sides of the story. It was to iron out these differences and arrive at the truth that Bryan conducted his long interviews and wrote his book.

In the end, Bryan's text actually exonerated Schwarzkopf from any kind of guilt—that is, outside the parameters of military action—and pictured him as an honorable and courageous officer.

Michael Mullen's mother, Peg Mullen, never did buy Bryan's absolution of Schwarzkopf. Eventually she planned to write her own book about the death of her son.

"Over the years," as Linda Rocawich wrote in *The Progressive*, Peg Mullen "got to know many men from her son's unit. . . . They fleshed out the story for her—the story of the night Michael died, and how, in the next several months, the battalion Schwarzkopf commanded took heavy casualties fighting in Cambodia many weeks before the official invasion."

Those friends of her son, Rocawich wrote in January 1991, "are wondering how many young men and women will die under his command in the Persian Gulf."

Seeds of dissatisfaction with his military life began to gnaw at Schwarzkopf because of this confrontation, even though he had always considered himself the quintessential officer. He found himself struggling to rein himself in when bungling politicians offended him, and he realized that the Vietnamese War was being wrongly presented to the public, certainly by much of the media. Besides that, there were no real military goals in the Vietnamese War. It was basically a war that America entered not to win, but to lose.

"Everyone who went to Vietnam and came home after it was over," Schwarzkopf said, "has had to come to his personal accommodation for that experience."

It was a kind of surgical operation for a cancerous growth. "When it's all over," Schwarzkopf told Bryan, "you've got the scar, number one; and number two, you're not really ever sure that you got it all out of your system. You never know when it's going to rear its ugly head again. But if you're going to live your life, you're going to have to learn to live with that.

"But I have to tell you, I was undergoing tremendous peaks and valleys to arrive at my own accommodation for my life. There were times when I was tempted to just bail out and go build myself a cabin in the wilderness and commune with nature."

Even Schwarzkopf knew that "communing with nature" was a kind of bizarre dream that he could never really imagine for himself under any circumstances.

He weathered the controversy over his actions in Vietnam eventually, but there were very hard moments in his life when he was going through the cleansing. Later on, his wife, Brenda, recalled Schwarzkopf's disappointment in 1970:

"When he came home from Vietnam, the second time, you know, it was very discouraging because there weren't any yellow ribbons or the red, white, and blue ribbons, and the flags waving."

He survived. There were traumas—traumas close to home. In a recent article for *The New Republic*, Bryan wrote of one of them. It was in the spring of 1972, Bryan said, the year before the last American troops left Vietnam. Lieutenant Colonel Schwarzkopf was then living in an Annandale apartment. He and Brenda were visited by Norman's sister Sally.

"My sister Sally—whom I love dearly, we are very, very close—came over one night with a magnum of excellent wine. And Sally and Brenda and I were consuming this vast quantity of wonderful wine and the TV was sort of on. It was the worst kind of war picture, totally contrived, with no realism in the whole thing."

Schwarzkopf kept his eye on the action. The soldiers had come to a mine field and were beginning to cross it.

"You just knew any damn minute some damn mine was going to go off, something you had been through a thousand times in real life, and all of a sudden the mine went off and people were blowing up in the mine field."

Schwarzkopf said that he found himself sitting there bathed in sweat.

"It was a terrible experience for me to see that, and my sister started asking me why I was having such an awful response."

Schwarzkopf tried to explain to her how he felt. He tried to explain the emotionalism that had gripped him, the flashback that had occurred in his psyche. He tried to communicate to her the depression he had experienced when he had returned home to find that whatever he had done in Vietnam was not appreciated by his loved ones and his friends.

"And then Sally, the sister whom I truly love, started saying, 'Well, you have to understand the other side of this thing.'"

It overwhelmed him that his own sister was opposed to the war in Vietnam. She began suggesting that the protesters demonstrating against the American presence in the war zone had a point. Maybe, even, they were right!

"And I *burst into tears!* Here was my own flesh and blood doubting. I was in tears that she could even *dare* to take the other side!"

And then he did a very Schwarzkopf-type of thing. He threw his sister—his own flesh and blood—he threw her bodily out of the apartment!

Sally burst into tears, too. "Why are you throwing me out of the house?" she asked him.

Schwarzkopf was yelling now. "Goddamn it! If you can even think that about our service there!"

And that was that.

The next morning cooler reason prevailed. Schwarzkopf knew he had been wrong in losing his temper. And even more wrong in giving way to his emotions by acting as he had.

He called up his sister and apologized. He admitted to her that he had been wrong, dead wrong, in what he had done. He knew she was entitled to her own opinion, even if it was contrary to his and even if it did impinge on his own ego. And she admitted that she was sorry, too.

It was a lesson to Schwarzkopf. It was a lesson in humility—and more than that. He read it correctly as his own anger, his own frustration, his own grief, and his own confusion about his work in Vietnam. He realized that if he let it, all this could in the end consume him with rage and a kind of self-destruction.

"I recognized that . . . whatever it was eating me away could absolutely destroy me if I didn't get a handle on it. In hindsight, from a personal, emotional standpoint, that was probably a major turning point for me."

In his conversations with C. D. B. Bryan, which were extensive during the research for *Friendly Fire*, Schwarzkopf had enunciated very clearly his feelings about fighting in Vietnam. He had been a soldier for fourteen years at the time he left Vietnam at the end of his second tour—having undergone both training and actual combat service.

"I volunteered for Vietnam the second time," he told Bryan,

"because I honestly felt I could be a better battalion commander, could accomplish the mission with less loss of life, than a lot of people who were going over there. I felt this because of the tremendous experience I had had fighting with the Vietnamese Airborne in 1965 and 1966.

"After my first tour, I came home with probably the greatest feeling of satisfaction I've ever had in anything I've ever done. I slept in the mud, ate rice and Vietnamese food with chopsticks for one solid year. Everywhere the Vietnamese went, I went. I was one of them. And I felt, I really felt, that I was honestly helping people.

"I met some fantastic people in that outfit, Vietnamese for whom I have the greatest respect in the world. These people were desperate. Many of them were from North Vietnam and had fled the communists in 1954. They were true patriots fighting for their country, for their lives! I came home that year feeling I had been fighting for freedom and democracy.

"When I volunteered for Vietnam in 1965, it was for 'God, Country, and Mom's Homemade Apple Pie.' I got to Vietnam, and we were surrounded at Dak To. Well, when you get surrounded and the sun goes down with you sitting there thinking you may not see it come up again the next morning, it takes a hell of a lot more than God, Country, and Mom's Apple Pie—those words emblazoned across the sky—to keep you going.

"I think we went to Vietnam in the first place for the principle of democracy. I'm not saying that that's what it all turned out to be, and I'm not saying that that was the end result. I'm saying only that this is the principle we went to Vietnam for."

As for himself, for what kept him going, he had a different reason.

"I had honestly met enough truly fine, dedicated South Vietnamese officers in the Vietnamese Airborne Division who sincerely and honestly believed that we were fighting for their country, for their freedom, and that I—as an American taught from the time I was knee-high to a grasshopper that one stands up and fights for democracy—that I was over there to help.

"Look, to go back over this whole business of why I volunteered a second time for Vietnam . . . to make my colonelcy—I didn't need any medals. I'd already been promoted ahead of my contemporaries by about a year. . . . I went to Vietnam sooner than most of my classmates, I went first as a captain/major and then again as a lieutenant colonel. Most of them, or many of them, had only been in Vietnam as majors.''

He pointed out that majors usually held staff positions. The highest officer commanding a company was usually a captain, with a lieutenant colonel in command of a battalion. He admitted, of course, that commanding a battalion was "career-enhancing."

"I would be foolish if I said I was unaware that commanding a battalion in Vietnam would help my career. Of course it would! But there were other things to consider.''

It hurt Schwarzkopf to realize that the Vietnam experience had generally been bad for the American people. In particular it hurt Schwarzkopf because it put him and the career in the military that he had chosen into the dustbin of public opinion.

"The public seems to have lost faith in the military because of the war in Vietnam. After all, we're only an arm of policy of the United States government. We're public servants. If the public no longer has confidence in us, then what good are we?

"I think right now in the officer corps there are an awful lot of people who feel confused about the public's attitude. I came into the army because I wanted to serve my country. I took an oath saying that I'd protect this country from all enemies foreign and domestic—I didn't say *I'd* determine who the enemies were! I said I'd merely protect the country after somebody else made that determination.

"So this war comes around in Vietnam; the duly elected government officials send us, the army, to fight the war. We go to Vietnam and fight the best way we know how—not needlessly wasting lives for the most part. We did the best we could, and it dragged on and on. Many of us were sent back a second time. A lot of young officers have been sent back a third time.''

And, of course, when they came home, they were derogated by their friends, their associates, and even their families in some cases. The demonstrations satisfied the demonstrators, apparently, Schwarzkopf thought, but it did the opposite to those being demonstrated against.

"Now this [kind of thing] is going to make me think long and hard before I go off to war again. This is me, Norm Schwarzkopf; personally, I don't think there will ever be another major confrontation where huge armies line up on both sides. If that happens, it's inevitably going to be nuclear weapons and the whole thing. God forbid, I hope we don't have any.

"War is a profanity. It really is. It's terrifying. Nobody is more antiwar than an intelligent person who's been to war. Probably the most antiwar people I know are my officers—but if we do have a war, I think it's going to be similar in nature to Vietnam and Korea. Limited in scope.

"And when they get ready to send me again, I'm going to have to stop and ask myself, 'Is it worth it?' That's a very dangerous place for the nation to be when your own army is going to stop and question."

There were other considerations that Schwarzkopf had found himself beginning to struggle with.

"What is moral?" he asked. "What is immoral? Where does duty stop and morality begin? Are we now saying that the military is supposed to question the morality of our government's commitment to a war?

"I don't know. I really don't know. If we allow the military to question whether or not to go, then it seems to me we also have to look at the other side of the coin. What if the government decides *not to go*? Do we allow the military the right to criticize this decision? To decide whether it was correct or not? And perhaps go to war in spite of the fact that the government decides we shouldn't?

"See, the military is required to follow the orders given it by the government. How they pursue it is another question—and here is where you get into civilian casualties, war crimes, atrocities, ovens, and all that business. If you're a member of the military, you don't really have much choice as far as pursuing the war or not. If it ever came to a choice between compromising my moral principles and the performance of my duties, I know I'd go with my moral principles.

"At the same time, however, I would also cease being an army officer. I would have to resign my commission. But even at that, I could be accomplishing my duty as I see it."

The Vietnam War caused a great deal of self-criticism about the military, indulged in mostly by the military itself.

Lessons were learned. And these lessons would come in handy in the next military operations engaged in.

If there ever were any.

8

Major General Schwarzkopf: Operation Urgent Fury

By the time C. D. B. Bryan's book, *Friendly Fire*, was published in 1976, H. Norman Schwarzkopf was in the process of being returned to peacetime duty in the army command. The last troops were out of Vietnam in March 1973 and the armed services were beginning to operate on a more normal, subdued basis.

The excesses and boners of the military were no longer the subject of the daily headlines. Like Schwarzkopf, most members of the top brass were taking a long, hard second look at their commands, particularly with a view to correcting some of the abuses that had surfaced during the long, arduous Vietnam years.

As for Schwarzkopf, he himself was happy to be able to spend a great deal more time with his family. He and Brenda had three children: Cynthia, the oldest, born in 1971, Jessica, born in 1973, and Christian, born in 1978.

There was no question about it: the two tours of duty in Vietnam had changed Schwarzkopf a great deal. No longer was he quite so gung-ho and free-wheeling. He had learned not only that things did not always go as planned but that the public perception of the armed services was at a brand-new low ebb, even for the United States, which had never really had any abiding faith or interest in its military arm. He was disturbed by it, but he knew that there was nothing he himself could do about it.

"In times of stress," he said, "you turn to the good Lord and to your family, and more than anything else, you call on that same inner strength that kept you going in a lot of other adverse times. It's not easy. But then you realize that's what you've been training for your entire life."

During this period of in-between—that is, in between service in Vietnam and service in the Persian Gulf War—Schwarzkopf was able to indulge himself in the things in life that he really loved to do. For example, he had always loved music, and by now he was an avid fan of the opera classics. He found the tension and emotion in the music and the singing to be a viable catharsis for his own nervous tensions.

In addition to listening to opera and watching action movies and television shows, he returned to another childhood passion: amateur magic. He had always loved to fool people, especially in making them watch something happening in the right hand when the essential trickery was being manipulated by the left hand. The idea was, of course, to be so good at forcing their attention to the innocent areas that there would be little reason for them to detect the hand that was, as the saying went, "quicker than the eye."

The saying, like many sayings, is, of course, untrue. It is not the hand that is quicker than the eye, it is the wit and attention-directing ability of the magician that directs the eye to another place so that the hand is out of sight at the critical moment.

Schwarzkopf instinctively knew that magic was a part of the trade he himself loved above all others—the trade of strategy and tactics in battle. And while he was resting now, he fine-tuned his own movements and repartee to keep the eye of the observer off the critical areas of the tricks he was performing.

The postings came and went. Once back in the States, he was assigned to command the 172nd Light Infantry Brigade, at Fort Greely, Arkansas. Soon enough he was shifted to Fort Lewis, Washington, where he was put in command of the 1st Brigade, 9th Infantry Division. In Germany he was assigned as assistant division commander of the 8th Infantry Division (Mechanized) of the United States Army in Europe.

On one happy instance, he was stationed in Alaska, where he stayed from 1974 to 1976. While there, he attended to the myriad of jobs any ranking officer handles, and found the recreational facilities in the area absolutely marvelous for a man of his outdoor interests.

It was there that he spent hours and days salmon fishing, and when he was not in his waders floundering through the white waters, he was out in the woods hunting. Sometimes he even took long hikes in Alaska's wild terrain. He would go with a group, or he would go alone.

His wife was with him, as was the family. They respected his love of the outdoors and his love of being by himself sometimes.

"It rained [one] weekend," Brenda recalled. "I went to pick him up, and he was sitting alongside the road with this smile on his face."

In 1983 he was ordered to Fort Stewart, Georgia, where he was made commander of the U.S. Army's premier "heavy" division, the 24th Infantry Division (Mechanized). This was one of the plums that occasionally fell off the tree. He made the most of it.

The between-wars quiet was not actually to last forever. It was broken for Schwarzkopf on Sunday evening, October 23, 1983. He had spent the day fishing for bass.

"I had promised a lot of people that I was a magnificent fisherman, and I hadn't caught very much fish since I'd been [at Fort Stewart]. So I came home and announced to my family, 'Eureka! Tonight I'm cooking dinner. I am going to take these bass and give you a beautiful Southern fried bass dinner with cornmeal.' "

Schwarzkopf was busy working in the kitchen, covering the bass with cornmeal, and had just put the first fillets in the frying pan when he heard the telephone ring. Brenda called him to the phone, announcing it was Atlanta calling. Although the suspicion of some possibility of action niggled at the corners of his mind, Schwarzkopf insouciantly announced his name into the mouthpiece and waited.

It was the Deputy Chief of Staff of Operations of the Armed Forces of the Atlantic Command. After a few words exchanged in small talk, the voice on the other end got down to business.

"What is it you think you're going to be doing for the next three weeks?"

Schwarzkopf knew instantly that something was in the wind. What it was, he had no idea. "Ever been asked a question like that?" Schwarzkopf asked rhetorically. "That really sets your head spinning very quickly."

Schwarzkopf gave a quick answer that really did not say anything, and then asked the operative: "Why?"

"You're probably not going to be doing that," said the voice. "You've been selected for a special mission."

Schwarzkopf nodded. "What am I going to be doing?"

There was a hesitation. "I can't tell you that."

"Where am I going to be?" Schwarzkopf asked, not to be put off entirely.

"I can't tell you that, either," said the voice. "But since I now know what your availability is, your selection has to be cleared. I'll call you back in a couple of hours and let you know."

And the line went dead.

Schwarzkopf was riveted there for a long moment. He knew, of course—or at least he *thought* he knew. That same morning, in Beirut, Lebanon, two hundred U.S. marines had been killed in their Beirut marine compound when a suicide bomb had been set off by a truck that rammed into the outer wall of the building.

"Suddenly I had no appetite at all. Every thought in my mind was Lebanon."

But it was *not* Lebanon. It was to be an entirely different operation in an entirely different theater of operations. On October 14, 1983, Maurice Bishop, the prime minister of the tiny island of Grenada in the Caribbean, had been put under house arrest. Later he was let go, and then rearrested. Actually, he had been executed by those taking over the government— but U.S. intelligence had not yet come up with that fact.

The revolutionaries were led by General Hudson Austin, the military commander of the island, and Bernard Coard, the radical deputy prime minister working under Bishop. For some time now, American intelligence had known that there were a number of Cuban construction workers—and no one knew how many of them were actually military advisers or even professional soldiers—working on a new airstrip on Grenada.

Even though Cuba had supported the deposed Maurice Bishop, it seemed logical to assume that this leftist takeover might be an action of some kind backed by the Cubans. No one knew how many, really, or if other Cubans would be coming onto the island to help maintain the new government.

On that same Sunday, the Organization of Eastern Caribbean States had contacted the United States, requesting help in seizing the forces of insurrection and restoring the proper government to Grenada—in addition to restoring order to the citizenry, who were at the time in wild disarray.

There were at the time about 1,100 American citizens on Grenada—over half of them college students at St. George's University School of Medicine, located at a town with the odd name of True Blue, just east of St. George, the capital of Grenada. The rest of the Americans were scattered throughout the tiny island.

Grenada was the southernmost of what was known as the Windward Islands, in the British West Indies. It was about eighty-five miles northwest of Trinidad—an oval-shaped island twenty-one miles long and only twelve miles wide. Discovered in 1498 by Christopher Columbus, it was originally named Conception. When the governor of Martinique, du Parquet, purchased the island in 1650, the French settled in it, managing to kill off most of the original population as they "civilized" the island.

Grenada was taken by the British in 1762 during the French-English wars in the second half of the eighteenth century, but it was recaptured by the French under Count d'Estaing in 1779, only to bounce back, ping-pong fashion, to Great Britain by the Treaty of Versailles in 1783, in whose possession it remained until February 7, 1974, when it became fully independent after a general strike against its British masters.

Schwarzkopf joined the operation to free Maurice Bishop and liberate Grenada shortly afterward when a second phone call came. The invasion of Grenada would be called Operation Urgent Fury. It had been in the planning stages for at least a week, shortly after the coup had been effected on October 14 by the house arrest of Bishop.

Because of the OECS request for help, the top U.S. brass—then called the Joint Special Operations Command (JSOC)—under General John Vessey, the Chairman of the Joint Chiefs of Staff, gave the go-ahead signal to invade in the early morning hours of October 25.

Schwarzkopf, now a two-star major general, was told that he would be engaged in an exercise that was predominantly in the hands of the navy. He would act as an adviser to the navy commander, Vice Admiral Joseph Metcalf III.

He was warned that the navy unfortunately felt no need for his presence in the operation and considered him an outsider. Nevertheless, he had been designated as deputy commander of Operation Urgent Fury. It would be his job to advise Admiral Metcalf on the use of the regular forces sent to Grenada.

There were three primary objectives to be met to secure the island of Grenada.

The first was to rescue—or at least assure the security of—the almost six hundred American students who were in residence and attendance at St. George's University School of Medicine at True Blue.

The second was to release from house arrest the governor-general of the island, Sir Paul Scoons, who had been captured at the time the prime minister had been taken.

The third was to capture the two revolutionaries who had deposed the government: General Hudson Austin, the military commander, and Bernard Coard, the deputy prime minister who had orchestrated the takeover.

These primary objectives were to be carried out by a number of special operations and a number of main-force operations. The special ops were to be handled by Delta Force paratroops and by Seal units.

Delta Force had been formed in the mid-seventies to act as counterterrorist and hostage-rescue units—devised to obviate forever a repetition of the botched-up "Eagle Claw" operation sent to Iran to free the U.S. hostages there in March 1980.

Delta Force operatives were usually airborne fighters trained in parachute landings and hand-to-hand combat.

The Seal units were primarily seagoing commandos, trained not only in counterterrorism at sea, but in reconnaissance missions of all kinds. They were actually a kind of supercommando force used in any kind of special operation desired.

Special operations for Delta Force included two specific jobs.

One was to seize the airstrip at Point Salines on the far eastern tip of the island, adjacent to the barracks where the Cuban construction units were housed. The field was to be reconnoitered in the early hours of morning, and seized just thirty minutes before the arrival of the main U.S. forces. Then it was to be cleared quickly of construction equipment left there by the Cubans after each day's work. The strip would then be operable for the main U.S. forces, which were to land and off-load there at dawn.

A second operation was to mount an assault against Richmond Prison—located not far from Government House in St. George, where it was supposed that the governor-general was lodged—to "rescue" from the prison any political prisoners who might be jailed as hostages of the revolutionary government.

The Seals had a number of jobs to do, including the liberation of the governor-general under house arrest, the evacuation of Scoons to the USS *Guam*, to destroy Radio Free Grenada now in the hands of the rebels, to reconnoiter the marine landing zone at Pearls Airport, and to take control of the island's main diesel generator plant near Grand Mal Bay.

The big attack would be carried out by the main forces. These would include Ranger forces and marines, and the 82nd Airborne Command. The regular-force missions would deliver the main blow against the island's defenders, and would include the 1st Ranger Battalion and the 2nd Ranger Battalion. The 2nd Ranger Battalion was already stationed at Fort Stewart, Georgia. The 1st Ranger Battalion was stationed at Fort Lewis, Washington, but would deploy to Fort Stewart for airlifting.

The main artillery arm would be the 82nd Airborne Division, which would deploy 3,000 men from Fort Bragg to the Point

Salines airstrip. A second brigade would be staged to Fort Bragg, to deploy as needed.

The regular-force missions were in the hands of Metcalf and Schwarzkopf. The two Ranger battalions contained about 1,600 men. The 82nd Airborne would airlift in 3,000 men in C-141 transports from Fort Bragg to Point Salines. The operation would include about 5,600 men at the height of the invasion.

Schwarzkopf recalled the situation in the early evening hours of October 24, the day before the invasion would start—as usual, at dawn. At the time he had just been airlifted onto the deck of Admiral Metcalf's command ship, and it was there that he took what stock he could of the situation.

"We were floating around somewhere out in the middle of the Caribbean, and we still didn't know if the Grenada rescue operation was going to take place," he recalled. "It was about 7 p.m. . . . [when] we got the orders to go. We sent messages out to everybody that, okay, it's a go, tomorrow morning at 5 a.m. it's going to happen."

Schwarzkopf thought about the coup that had occurred on the island, and about the installation of the revolutionary head of state, and he thought about the Americans on the island— a lot of college-age kids, and adults trying to conduct their daily businesses. And he thought of the Cubans, who might or might not be behind the coup.

"And I went out and I was standing on the flight deck, and the ship was kind of tossing a little bit, the wind was blowing in my face, and I thought, *Grenada!* The United States of America is about to launch a military operation into Grenada and I'm involved."

He was back in the thick of the action, and once again, he felt certain, controversy would reign. People would be looking slantwise at the military again, maybe hating it the way they had Vietnam. Still—

"And, of course, a lot of the Vietnam memories came rushing back. What am I getting into here? Why is the U.S. going into Grenada? What are we doing? What are our strategic interests in Grenada?

"And then I thought, 'Hey, Schwarzkopf'—and you will probably never believe this, but I thought of that conversation

[C. D. B. Bryan and I] had had years ago about 'immoral wars' and whether an army officer should stand up and say this is an immoral war and, therefore, I choose not to fight this one.''

He was close to examining it from every angle, close to wondering exactly *what* he was fighting—

''And I thought, this is sort of the bottom line, the very crux of the difference between being an army officer and being in some other line of work.'' He stood there on the deck and he thought, ''I took an oath that said I would obey the lawful orders of my commanding officers, one of whom is the President of the United States.''

He had been in the army twenty-seven years at the time. He had had his salary paid and his family clothed, he had had a roof over his head, and he had risen to the rank of major general.

''Do I now have an option to say, 'Hey, before I commit myself to this thing, I'd like to talk about it a bit more'?''

Did he? Of course he did not.

''I didn't really know [what we were getting into]. I knew we were going in to free the [American] students. But I didn't know how we were going to be greeted by the Grenadan people. I certainly didn't know how the American people were going to take it. Or Congress.''

But he had answered that telephone call. And he had been flown out to the deck of the flagship.

''My orders were very clear to me, and I honestly don't think you have the right as an army officer to consider that you have an option.''

In the end, he did the job.

Complicated though the job was, it succeeded—with a number of odd quirks and strange glitches. At least, it worked for Schwarzkopf. He had come aboard as a total stranger to Vice Admiral Metcalf. However, by the time the invasion had come to a conclusion two days later, he had so impressed Metcalf that he had undergone a metamorphosis from uninvited guest to Metcalf's friend.

''The object [of the operation] was to go in with what really started as a relatively unconventional operation,'' Schwarzkopf said, looking back on it later. "It was going to be quick in, quick and dirty: we were going to isolate the two airfields, we were going to get in on top of all those critical buildings [the government buildings, the radio station, the prison where Bishop was believed held], take them all, and say, 'That's it, it's over with.' "

Quick in, quick out. Surgical. Precise.

Sure.

"And at the end of Day One," Schwarzkopf recalled ruefully, "the whole exercise was going to be done. But what started as a highly unconventional, surgical-in-nature operation went sour *right away*. And it went sour because of the assumption that the Cubans weren't going to fight. We had eight hundred Cubans on the island who were well armed and damned sure *were* going to fight."

It had been thought that the antiaircraft weapons would be largely ineffective and that helicopter movement would run as smooth as silk. It had been thought that the guns on the island were old-fashioned quad–30mms, manned by amateur gunners with poor morale.

The invading American forces soon learned to their dismay that the gunners were trained soldiers, highly disciplined, and courageous. They remained at their posts and fired back, in the face of heavy onslaught. The special missions did not always succeed. When the main-force fighting men were parachuted in, they were fired upon heavily.

Schwarzkopf had no excuses. He knew everyone would be looking at him and saying: "My God, you ended up with six thousand Americans in there and only eight hundred Cubans! It seems to me you should have rolled over them!"

Yes. That was true. "If it had been a *conventional* battle, where we were using artillery, fighting conventional tactics without regard to civilian casualties and collateral damage, we probably would have.

"I could have rolled into Grenada with my mechanized armor divisions, my overwhelming division artillery; I could have hit the beach with LSTs, rolled my tanks off, cranked up my artillery, and blown St. George's off the map.

"I could have had the whole thing tied up in a neat little

bundle in an hour, maybe an hour and a half. But that wasn't the nature of the operation, and it obviously would have been a terrible thing to do."

Although the Grenada invasion, with all its snafus—and they were *legion*—all its problems, was in the end a political success, and an operation that went down in the books as a U.S. victory, it did rankle in many minds. Two newspapermen, Richard Gabriel and Paul Savage, wrote a study of the invasion in the *Boston Globe*. "What really happened in Grenada," they wrote, "was a case study in military incompetence and poor execution."

They cited instances in which officers wanted to bring charges of cowardice against pilots who panicked, only to have superiors "counsel" them not to press the issue. They cited a thirty-five-man special-operations group that lost ten men who were never included in the official death count of twenty because the Pentagon wanted to keep the group's existence secret. They cited a "panic" that resulted in three-fourths of a force that was supposed to parachute into Grenada never having been airlifted from Fort Stewart, Georgia, but listened to the war on their pocket radios!

"Some families of dead servicemen have also recently telephoned Washington journalists to say they believe they have convincing evidence that their sons died in combat recently, rather than in accidents described by the Pentagon. These families have been unable, however, to make ironclad cases and some have withdrawn their remarks, saying they had been told to 'shut up' by the Pentagon."

Richard Gabriel, who cowrote the foregoing criticism of the operation for the *Boston Globe*, eventually published a book titled *Military Competence: Why the American Military Doesn't Win*, in which an analysis of the Grenada invasion, as well as an analysis of the aborted Iran rescue mission, is included.

A House subcommittee later studied the invasion, and in the mid-eighties released the record of a closed hearing on classified Defense Department documents. It found that "the mission was fraught with confusion brought on mainly by hasty planning." In conclusion, "An almost total lack of intelligence data about the situation on the island . . . was followed by critical failures of military communication and faulty tactics.''

Nevertheless, when Major General H. Norman Schwarzkopf came back from the Caribbean, he was happy to see that a small group had gathered at the airfield to welcome him. The band was there. Brenda and the children were there. His enlisted aide was there, and some of the men he shot skeet with were there with their wives and children.

''Johnny was coming home from war again and I had expected to come home just the same way I came home from war the last two times; no big deal. It was going to be routine. But when the airplane landed, the band was out there, and there were big signs saying WELCOME HOME and I walked out of the airplane and everybody started cheering and my wife and kids ran up and hugged me, and I didn't understand what was going on! Isn't that crazy? Do you see what I'm saying? But I've got to tell you, when it finally dawned on me, it was probably one of the greatest thrills I have ever had in my entire life.''

Even if it was a balls-up, the invasion of Grenada was generally conceded by the public to be a brilliant success. It was that—a brilliant public-relations success. Shortly after it was over, Major General Schwarzkopf was elevated to the rank of Lieutenant General Schwarzkopf—joining the fairly small and prestigious number of three-star generals in the United States.

9

Major General Powell: The Iran-Contra Affair

It was never widely known that Major General Colin L. Powell was one of only sixteen select people in the U.S. government to know of the Iran-Contra scandal while it was in progress. The name of Colin L. Powell was third on a list drawn up by Lieutenant Colonel Oliver North, indicating "people who know" about the U.S. government's secret dealings with Iran.

Only Secretary of State George P. Shultz and Defense Secretary Caspar W. Weinberger preceded Powell's name on the list. In 1986, few people in the country had even heard of Powell, let alone knew of his direct involvement in the affair that later became known as the Iran-Contra scandal.

Remarkably enough, Powell's involvement in the full-blown scandal did not damage his career at all. If anything, it accelerated his rise in Washington.

In the 427-page majority congressional report on the Iran-Contra affair, Powell's name was mentioned less than six times.

The story of Iran-Contra started in 1985 when Admiral Poindexter, who was head of the National Security Council, asked Powell to furnish him with information about the pricing and availability of TOW antitank missiles, whose destination was Iran, via Israeli middlemen. The missiles were to be exchanged for American hostages held in Lebanon by Islamic fanatics closely allied with Iran.

Powell told *The Washington Post* on March 23, 1987, "I provided the information to the National Security Council, a routine service that I would provide to any department."

According to another story in *The Washington Post*, dated December 16, 1987, "Powell [had also] acted as a coordinator for the Pentagon in the November 1985 Israeli shipment of Hawk missiles to Iran . . . prior to [that] shipment. Powell had been active on behalf of Weinberger in opposing arms deals with Iran."

Later Powell became actively involved in the Iran-Contra affair in January 1986, when President Reagan authorized arms sales to Iran. The previous shipment by way of the Israelis had not been authorized by Reagan. Powell now became the person, according to Weinberger, whom Weinberger "used to carry out the President's directions."

Powell actually implemented the arms sales to Iran in 1986. He was one of only five people in the Pentagon who knew of the covert deal, according to his own testimony before congressional committees in camera. He was never charged with any misconduct, and won praise when it was discovered he had asked Poindexter in a memo whether he should legally notify Congress about the arms deal or not. Poindexter never answered his query.

Powell was serving under Weinberger as a military aide when the Iran-Contra deal took place. As a matter of fact, Weinberger himself opposed the arms-for-hostages scheme.

It was Powell who dealt with the CIA when the agency asked the Pentagon to lay on a shipment of four thousand TOW missiles. Powell gave the CIA request to Lieutenant General Vincent M. Russo, the CIA contact at the Department of Defense.

He then contacted General Maxwell R. Thurman, vice chief of staff of the army, and told him to prepare, sub rosa, four thousand missiles for transfer to the CIA, whence they would be consigned to Iran.

Partially because of the surreptitiousness of the deal and

partly because of lax army bookkeeping, the wrong TOW missiles were sent. The army was supposed to send basic TOWs that sold for $3,469 apiece. Instead, somebody marked down the wrong stock numbers on the order and the army wound up sending an advanced version of the TOW priced at $8,435 apiece.

Lieutenant Colonel Oliver North's middleman firm ponied up the lower price for the TOWs and then charged the buyers for the higher-priced models, the ones actually sent to Iran. In this manner, the middleman firm reaped a huge profit.

When asked if he should have handled the Iran-Contra affair differently, Powell replied:

"I'm very comfortable with the role I performed in this transaction. It was correct and adequate to the circumstances. I've got no second thoughts about that. . . . A correct instruction had been received by the Secretary of Defense that was legally sufficient, and we were executing that instruction."

The fact that he did not blow the whistle on the Iran-Contra deal was in keeping with his views of government secrecy, which he explained when he became National Security Adviser in 1987.

"I will keep secret that which needs to remain secret, and I'll tell you to your face that I'm not going to tell you something. But when it's appropriate, I will be as available as the circumstances seem to dictate."

In other words, Powell would not act like Poindexter, who headed the National Security Council in 1985 and deliberately gave the White House press office misinformation. Poindexter even attempted to spread disinformation about Libya through the news media and denied that America would invade Grenada moments before it did so. Poindexter called the invasion "preposterous."

Instead of lying like Poindexter, Powell said he would have handled the situation by not saying anything.

In the Iran-Contra affair, Poindexter came off as a kind of rogue elephant, whereas Powell earned the reputation of a trusted team player. Poindexter's career went by the boards; Powell's surged to new heights. Powell was one of the few participants in the scandal who walked away from it with his reputation clean.

In June 1986 Powell became the commanding general of the 5th Corps, composed of 72,000 troops in Frankfurt, Germany. Here he got a temporary promotion to lieutenant general—that is, three-star general.

Six months later Frank Carlucci, the newly appointed National Security Adviser, called Powell into his office and asked him to work for him as his deputy in the White House. Powell, who was happy in his job as commanding general of the 5th Corps, respectfully declined the appointment. He said he preferred military duties to politics. Carlucci did not give up easily. He continued to deluge Powell with calls, asking him to take on the job as Carlucci's deputy. Powell continued to stand firm in his negative stance.

Finally President Reagan himself called Powell with the same request. That settled it. Powell finally said yes. How could he refuse a request from the Commander in Chief of the armed forces?

As Carlucci's deputy, Powell explained the way he liked to run the National Security Council. "Like Frank, I am a great believer that the interagency process works best when everybody has a chance to say his piece and get his positions out on the table . . . that when we forward the final decision package to the President or present it to him orally, everybody who played knows he has been properly represented and had his day in court."

In his new job, Powell was the head of the Policy Review Group in the National Security Council. This was a high-level interagency committee composed of members of the CIA, the Defense and State Departments, and other undersecretary departments.

The group met at the White House two or three times a week to collect information about national security glitches, hash out approaches to be undertaken, and come to interagency agreements. The group dealt with such problems as Central America, Afghanistan, and the Middle East. Just above the Policy Review Group was the National Security Planning Group, consisting of the President, his National Security Adviser, and cabinet officers in charge of defense and foreign topics. One of the jobs of this group was to review Powell's Policy Review Group.

According to one official who participated in both groups, Carlucci and Powell worked as a team. "Frank provides the muscle, and Colin is orchestrator of decisions. . . . They're very comfortable working together."

Powell reorganized the NSC staff along the lines recommended by the Tower Commission, which President Reagan put together to get to the bottom of the Iran-Contra scandal. Under Poindexter, the National Security Council had been compartmentalized like the CIA, so that no one really knew what anyone else on the staff was doing.

That was all changed under Powell's ministry. He reorganized the National Security Council along clear lines of authority. He assigned responsibilities with regard to functional and geographical areas, and he had all involved parties participate in the dialogue.

As chairman of the Policy Review Group, Powell carried on his main task of screening out proposals that had little chance of approval by the President. He called these wacky proposals "pet rocks" and tossed them out before the President could even get a glimpse of them.

While he was in the National Security Council, he lobbied hard for the military. For instance, when the Iranians harassed commercial shipping in the Persian Gulf, Powell pushed for an increased American presence there. *The Washington Post* in its November 2, 1987, issue said that this "led to the controversial decision to reflag Kuwaiti oil tankers and deploy an American armada in the region."

Powell preferred this to a rigid, open organization in the NSC because he wanted to avoid the errors generated by the Iran-Contra affair. The problem with the NSC at that time was that such a small number of members knew of the Iran-Contra deal that the deal was never properly discussed among its members.

As Powell explained it, "I'm not a great believer in restricting attendance. I prefer to have the right people at a meeting even if the meeting tends to get a little large. I'm not a great slammer of doors.''

Robert B. Sims, a one-time press spokesman at the Pentagon and the White House, described Powell as "sophisticated and realistic about how Congress and the press fit into things." Also, Powell was "someone who believes in making the system work; he believes in working with people, not against them." And, "[Powell] is extremely articulate, and he sees the value of working with the press and with Congress to generate policy support."

Carlucci had so much faith in Powell that he would send Powell alone to confer with President Reagan, even though it was a matter of course that the National Security Adviser himself, *not* his deputy, was to brief the President daily.

Marlin Fitzwater, President Reagan's spokesperson, said that Reagan "has the highest respect and affection for General Powell. It was the general . . . who helped restructure and give new direction to the National Security Council following the Iran-Contra investigation, and who, by his personal integrity and commitment, has restored confidence in the National Security Council itself."

Powell once said of his NSC job, "I'm principally a broker. I have strong views on things, but my job is to make sure the President gets the best information available to make an informed decision."

Like Dirty Harry, Powell believes that a good man knows his limitations. He is also a man who knows exactly what he is about—always. In one interview he said: "I wasn't hired to be a grand strategist. I have no pretensions of being a Henry Kissinger or Zbigniew Brzezinski. I was not hired for that. Nor is that my background." He also said, "I was hired by Frank Carlucci in the first instance to help reestablish confidence . . . in the NSC system and . . . to fix something which, at that time, was seen to be broken. We had a plan, we executed that plan, and we were rather successful in putting that process back on a firm footing."

Powell maintained that the purpose of his role in the NSC was "to put in perspective the advice [the President] receives from other advisers. Where I think my advice is better . . . I provide it to the President, but I always try to let the other advisers know I'm doing that because I like to see a collegial operation.''

His qualities of efficiency, loyalty, levelheadedness, and political astuteness made him a perfect broker at the NSC.

When Powell actually became the head of the National Security Council, he lambasted the officials who used to run the NSC during the Iran-Contra scandal. He said, simply, that the NSC had been restored as a ''moral operation.'' After all, it was the NSC that directed the U.S. missile sales to Iran and then laundered the profits through numbered Swiss bank accounts to the Nicaraguan Contras.

''We run an operation that I feel is accountable to the President and administration, Congress and the American people,'' he went on to say. ''Everything we do at the NSC has to be in the name of the American people in the furtherance of their foreign policy as set by the President of the United States. . . . We have restored that level of confidence and honesty to the NSC.''

Fielding a question from a reporter who asked if Powell agreed with Oliver North's statement that sometimes lying to Congress was justified to protect national security, Powell said, ''No, and no. I do not believe a public official under the oath and having sworn an oath to the Constitution and the people of the United States has any part in any set of circumstances to lie, either to Congress or to the press.

''I've never done it. I never will do it. If I can't say something because it is a secret, I also have an obligation to protect the people's secrets. I will say, 'I can't tell you.' I do not believe it is the responsible course of action for public officials to lie, dissemble, or in some way deceive.''

Admitting there were arguments and bureaucratic infighting in his National Security Council, he told the *Christian Science Monitor*: ''We still have internecine battles. I've never seen a family that does not. But where we have disagreements, disagreements are good. Creative tension in an organization is good. You tend to get the best out of people. What we've tried to do is put in place a process and a system that deals with that tension and with those disagreements in a way that is focused internally.

"So that when the President makes his decision, everybody feels that they have played in the process, they have presented their view to the President, and now we're going to execute the President's foreign policy, not the National Security Adviser's foreign policy or the Secretary of State's or the Secretary of Defense's."

He was right on track. In point of fact, the National Security Council was established in 1947 to coordinate the various agencies of government, such as the Pentagon and the State Department, with the goal of hammering out a cohesive policy.

To keep the council running smoothly, Powell poured oil on troubled waters during the meetings.

"One of the reasons you have leaks breaking out and people fighting out issues in public is when they don't think decisions are going to be made inside," Powell explained. "But if you have an orderly decision process, and decisions are made, and they're made fairly promptly, you have a better opportunity to have an orderly in-house system rather than a public shouting match."

Since he was the first black to hold the position of National Security Adviser, Powell felt "privileged" about taking the post. He assumed the position on November 5, 1987, when Reagan promoted him to it. The job was left open when Caspar Weinberger suddenly decided to resign for personal reasons—mainly because of his wife's poor health.

It was Weinberger and Howard Baker, the White House Chief of Staff, who immediately conferred with President Reagan. Reagan accepted Weinberger's decision to resign, and then the three of them discussed a successor—in effect, who should become Secretary of Defense.

Weinberger favored William Taft IV, his deputy. Baker favored Frank Carlucci, the National Security Adviser. Baker prevailed, and Carlucci became Secretary of Defense.

They then fell to talking about filling the vacancy they had just created—National Security Adviser. The person who holds the job guides the National Security Council staff and gives the President a thirty-minute briefing every morning.

Fred Barnes in *The New Republic* once called the job in the Reagan years "Reagan's Bermuda Triangle" because it was "swallowing up more appointees than any other job in his administration."

The first name suggested was Major General Colin L. Powell. He had been Deputy National Security Adviser for ten months already.

The President agreed wholeheartedly. "Nobody else was considered," Baker said later.

According to Barnes, Reagan "stumbled onto the kind of National Security Adviser he always needed but never had, a tough guy without an independent streak."

One of Powell's chief jobs as National Security Adviser was to try to obtain military aid for the Contras, who were trying to depose the Sandinista government in Nicaragua. In his new position, Powell did not dream up another Iran-Contra deal. He had already seen how it had toppled Poindexter from his throne of power.

Congressional leaders were pleased with Powell's above-board tactics to win aid for the Contras. There were dissenters, of course; unanimity is rare in Congress. Some congressmen believed Powell went too far in January 1988, when he exhorted the leaders of Guatemala, El Salvador, Costa Rica, and Honduras to denounce Nicaragua, thereby influencing an upcoming vote on Contra aid in Congress.

Powell warned the Central American leaders that if they helped stamp out the Contras, the U.S. government's financial aid to their countries might suddenly dry up.

He failed to persuade Congress to pass Reagan's $36,250,000 aid request for the Contras by a margin of merely eight votes in the House on February 3, 1988.

As Fred Barnes pointed out, Powell succeeded at least six National Security Advisers appointed by Reagan. He succeeded Richard Allen, William Clark, Robert McFarlane, John Poindexter, Alton Keel (acting), and Frank Carlucci. Reagan was unhappy with all of them save for Carlucci and Powell.

The fact that Powell was avidly pro-Contra might have helped make him appeal to Reagan. Powell was strong enough to handle policy squabbles in the NSC, but he wasn't so pow-

THE NEW AMERICAN HEROES 97

erfully strong that he initiated—or wanted to—any operations like a second Iran-Contra deal.

Said Powell: "I have strong views on things, but my job is to make sure the President gets the best information available to make an informed decision. I am not here for the purpose of lining up against Shultz or against Carlucci or against [CIA Director William] Webster."

He has said of the job: "I have an insatiable demand to be in charge of the information flow. If you don't know what information is flowing through your organization, you don't know what's going on in your organization."

Assistant Secretary of Defense Richard Armitage lauded Powell's NSC with the following words: "The leadership of the NSC before [the Iran-Contra scandal] was tumultuous. Now, when I go to a policy review, I *know* the Defense Department is going to get its issue on the table."

As Reagan's National Security Adviser, Powell arranged three Reagan-Gorbachev summit meetings as well as four other important international meetings. Powell countenanced the belief that the U.S. government should never cut deals with terrorists. He did not want another Iran-Contra scandal on his hands.

10

Lieutenant General Powell: Noriega, Hussein, and Gorbachev

At the beginning of the Panama crisis in late 1989, General Powell did not support a U.S. military action against dictator Manuel Antonio Noriega. What Powell wanted was to offer a deal to Noriega that would have him step down from power in exchange for the U.S.'s dropping of federal drug-smuggling indictments against him.

Would this be considered a "deal" with a terrorist? Powell wondered. In the end, he never had to make a decision on that question. The offer cut no ice.

Secretary of State George Shultz and the Assistant Secretary of State for Latin America, Elliott Abrams, wanted to drive Noriega out of Panama by using more forceful measures. Powell disagreed. He figured it would be all but impossible to oust Noriega. On the CBS show *Nightwatch*, Powell said of the man: "He has proved to be very persistent. I always thought he would be."

After the Reagan administration imposed sanctions on Panama, Powell believed they would have no effect on Noriega. "Ten days from now, he'll still be there," he told one of his aides. Powell never thought it very important to topple Noriega from power in the first place. Such a goal he felt to be unrealistic.

Shultz persisted in dreaming up plans to force Noriega out of power, and Powell persisted in rejecting them. Shultz wanted to send two combat brigades into Panama to take care of the dictator. Then he wanted to kidnap Noriega. Then he wanted to install deposed Panamanian President Eric Arturo Delvalle in the Canal Zone as leader of a government in exile. Then he wanted to set up a TV station that would broadcast Delvalle's speeches to Panama.

Reagan could not get excited about any of Shultz's proposals. Powell was subtle about his opposition to them. He had other members of the NSC object to them for him. A senior White House official at the time explained how Powell's modus operandi worked:

"The minute Shultz's views were put on the table in an open NSC meeting, they were knocked down by everybody."

Powell opposed Shultz's State Department plans elsewhere. He sided with the hard-liners against Shultz on the topic of Afghanistan, for example. Powell wanted Reagan's presummit speech in Springfield, Massachusetts, to criticize the Soviets about their invasion of Afghanistan. Shultz wanted the criticism deleted from the speech.

In the end Powell won. The speech claimed that the Soviets "still hope to prop up their discredited, doomed puppet regime, and they still seek to pose a threat to neighboring Pakistan, to whom we have a long-standing commitment."

When Soviet leader Mikhail Gorbachev found out about the speech, he complained bitterly to Shultz in Moscow several days later.

That was not the first time Shultz and Powell disagreed on policy. When he worked for NSC's Carlucci, Powell found himself at odds with Secretary of State Shultz on the subject of arms-reduction talks with the Soviets. Shultz wanted to move faster on arms reduction, Powell slower.

In a tense meeting with Carlucci and Shultz, Powell, siding with Carlucci, said, "George, some of your people want to give away the store. The President isn't going to do it." Powell had powerful friends at the White House at this time, namely Weinberger, Carlucci, and White House Chief of Staff Howard H. Baker, Jr.

It was during his stint as National Security Adviser that Powell first encountered Iraq's Saddam Hussein. At this time the U.S. was helping Hussein oppose Iran's Ayatollah Ruhollah Khomeini during the Iran-Iraq war. In fact, the U.S. was providing anti-Iranian intelligence to Iraq.

As Powell explained it, "At the time our objectives were to see that we could continue to maintain freedom of navigation in the Persian Gulf."

Powell liked neither Iran nor Iraq. He was said to agree with Henry Kissinger's great line: "Too bad they both can't lose."

Powell was worried that Iran might win the war and as a result obtain too much power in the Persian Gulf region. His policy was to play Iraq off against Iran lest Iran, which called America the "Great Satan," became a too-formidable power.

In order to pursue this policy, Powell said, "We tried to maintain neutrality. That was our stated policy, and it was the policy we executed. Over time, it helped produce a cease-fire. But I don't think any of us had any misgivings or illusions about what Mr. Saddam Hussein was like or what he was all about. We didn't see him as a God-fearing democratic leader waiting to burst out at the first opportunity. But you play the cards you're dealt at the time you're dealt them."

As National Security Adviser, Powell worked a twelve-hour day, from 7 a.m. to 7 p.m., and was swamped with offers to receive honorary degrees and special honors, along with invitations to speak. Powell never had any time for them because of his heavy schedule. He also was responsible for delivering a half-hour written briefing each day to the President.

In December 1987 General Powell warned the Soviet Union against distributing advanced weaponry to Nicaragua. Nicaragua was always a thorn in the side of the Reagan administration. Powell was responding to Nicaraguan Defense Minister Humberto Ortega's speech that he was going to double the size of his military forces. He claimed the U.S. government was planning an all-out invasion of Nicaragua.

Powell termed Ortega's speech "incredible." On ABC-TV's

This Week with David Brinkley, Powell said, "We would view such an introduction of advanced Soviet weaponry into the region a very serious matter. I wouldn't want to say what we might . . . do at the time that it happened. We would view this kind of intrusion of this kind of weaponry into our hemisphere with the greatest seriousness."

Referring to the October 1983 U.S. invasion of Grenada, Ortega had said, "With what [military strength] we have now, the gringos have something to think about. This is not Grenada. Here it will not be the same."

Powell had an answer. "I think one has to look at why a nation of three million people would want to have 600,000 people under arms. I think this presents a direct threat to their neighbors. It also clearly is a good way to keep control of the political situation when you put most of the military-age males under military power."

As National Security Adviser, Powell remained suspicious of the Soviets. On November 29, 1988, he said, "Despite the progress we have made with the Soviets, we cannot speak of shared values or partnership." He hooted at Gorbachev's call for a "common European home."

He went on. "The Soviets assure us that there would be room in this house for the United States and Canada as well. We appreciate the reassurance. But we did not ask for it nor do we need it. We are in Europe not at the invitation of the Soviet Union but in alliance with our Western allies." He added that NATO was the "hallmark of the Reagan presidency."

Carrying his suspicion of the USSR further, Powell said of Gorbachev's "new political thinking," "Are we witnessing a new creation, and if so, shall we actively participate in it? Has the phrase 'the Soviet threat' lost all meaning for the West?

"I think not.

"We are told to be patient; such radical changes take time. Patient we will be; but we must also be persistent and prudent. Our readiness to negotiate with the Soviets must be matched by our readiness to keep our forces modernized."

Powell ended his speech with, "If we analyze what this Soviet-built home would contain, we find some very old ideas indeed: unbalanced disarmament proposals, dissolution of military alliances, removal of foreign bases, and acceptance—yes, acceptance—of the ideological division of Europe presently enforced by Soviet power.

"Can this common European home enhance collective security? Can it ease East-West tensions? The answer to both questions is clearly no."

A few weeks earlier, in a speech to the American Stock Exchange Conference on U.S. Perspectives, Powell had praised Gorbachev but had doubts nonetheless. Powell said the U.S. "must nevertheless reserve judgment on both his economic goals and how he intends to achieve them.

"It is the failure of past Soviet policies—because there was effective resistance to their aggression—that led the Soviets to reassess those policies.

"Will perestroika, to paraphrase words used in our election campaign, lead to a kinder, gentler Soviet Union? What advice should the U.S. government give its businessmen who wish to compete in the Soviet Union?

"These are tough questions. We cannot forget that our overall relationship continues to be both competitive and adversarial. This is unlikely to change within our lifetimes."

Powell added, "The Soviet Union shows no evidence as yet of changing its basic military force structure, its emphasis on expanding and modernizing its weapons systems, or its aggressive, illegal program for acquiring strategic technologies.

"Until the Soviets can establish convincingly that it has made significant changes in these areas, it is not in our interest to change our policy."

When asked if he thought Gorbachev was seeking world domination, Powell answered, "As a personal matter, I don't think he does that. I think he is fully committed to a political philosophy that has that as its original and continuing goal, but I think it's a goal that he knows is not achievable."

Powell also said there were good things about Gorbachev's Soviet Union:

"Another factor that has to be taken into account, I believe, is the constructive role that is increasingly being played by the Soviet Union in resolving regional crises. Political and economic change in the Soviet Union . . . is contributing to an improved international climate that presents new opportunities to settle differences.

"But, the basic lesson I would leave you with is that strength and resolve on the part of the West is what helped us to set the stage for all the developments I have just described. It is the failure of past Soviet policies because there was effective resistance to aggression that led the Soviets to reassess those policies.

"This is no time to lower our guard or relax our vigilance. On the contrary, if the Soviets are really at a historic crossroads, it is all the more essential for us to foreclose, once and for all, any temptation they may still have to challenge the international system."

But "we can applaud Mr. Gorbachev for his realistic appraisal of the problems of the Soviet economy, and we can encourage him to recognize the policy implications of this appraisal. But we must nevertheless reserve judgment on both his economic goals and how he intends to achieve them."

Gorbachev's "real challenge is to try to face the challenges that the Soviet Union is going to be facing in the 1990s and in the twenty-first century for the advent of technology and the aggressiveness of market-based economies such as ourselves, and he [is] saddled with the political philosophy that does not turn loose the creative energies of his people.

"He recognizes that, in my judgment, as his fundamental problem, and he has come upon the concept of glasnost and perestroika to try to deal with that. And I just don't know how successful he will be with these two new concepts, saddled with a political philosophy that, in my judgment, is bankrupt, and not up to the challenge of the twenty-first century."

Later on in the speech he denounced South Africa's apartheid. This was in keeping with his long-standing hatred of racism that he had always felt was rife in corporate America.

Said Powell, "South Africa and their form of government or social control known as apartheid is an abomination on the face of the earth. It has to go. It will go. The same historical forces which are at work elsewhere in the world are at work in South Africa.

"We have policy debates here in Washington and within

the alliance as to how best to move that process along and there are the usual debates as to whether economic sanctions and boycotts help the government and hurt the blacks of South Africa more so than move the process along. So we have these debates, but the commitment is absolutely intact and the President has reaffirmed it on many an occasion.''

This from the man whom some blacks accuse of being too cautious when it comes to the topic of racism! Actually, Powell had gotten down to brass tacks many times in speeches addressing racism and how much he detested it. He once said he ''wish[ed] that there were other activities in our society . . . as open as the military is to upward mobility, to achievement, to allowing them in. I wish that corporate America, I wish the trade unions around the nation, would show the same level of openness and opportunity to minorities.''

Powell declared at a dinner of the Joint Center for Political and Economic Studies, ''The struggle [against racism] will not be over until every American is able to find his or her own place in our society, limited only by his or her own ability.''

All in all, Powell had a shining career as National Security Adviser. It was capped off with the Distinguished Service Award presented to him by Secretary of State George Shultz for Powell's work on a U.S.-Soviet arms control agreement and the Moscow summit.

In a surprise ceremony in the Secretary of State's office, Shultz gave Powell the award, which was a plaque and two medals.

All of which was pretty amazing, considering the fact that Powell was virtually unknown outside military circles two years before in 1986. What was more, the spectacularly quick rise of Powell's star did not stop at the position of National Security Adviser. Some commentators attributed his rise to powerful friends in powerful jobs, others to his intelligence and hard work—plus lucky breaks, of course.

Powell held court in the job in a manner markedly different from Henry Kissinger, who had the post under President Nixon, and Zbigniew Brzezinski, who held it under President Carter. These two National Security Advisers reported only to the President. Powell, on the other hand, reported to the President, the Secretary of State, the Secretary of Defense, and the Vice President, as all these men are statutory members of the National Security Council.

Explained Powell, "I'm the staff director for the NSC, not just the President, and I take that very seriously. My first responsibility is to make sure they're all served. Then I put on my other hat as assistant to the President and get into fights with them."

Powell set the tone for national security meetings, according to Frank Carlucci, who said of Powell, "He does it in a way that doesn't say, 'I, Colin Powell, am telling you you can't do this,' but rather, 'This is just the way the situation is here in the White House.' He never, never usurps the authority of the President. But the position is always so well-reasoned that by and large he carries the day."

One of his toughest jobs as National Security Adviser was in winning financial aid for the Contras in Nicaragua. Congress inevitably voted against him, even though Powell warned:

"A Sandinista victory over the democratic resistance would have ominous consequences for freedom inside Nicaragua and for the peace and security of all of Nicaragua's neighbors. Unless Congress and the President—which means ultimately the American people—come to agreement on a program of effective aid for the Nicaraguan resistance as an adjunct to our diplomatic strategy, the next President will probably face a situation of accelerating deterioration, as all the local democracies will come under growing strains as Nicaragua grows stronger, more assertive, and more aggressive."

The Contra issue was the most divisive foreign policy issue during the Reagan administration. Powell told the Los Angeles World Affairs Council in July 1988 that "when we are united— as we have been in support of the Afghan freedom fighters, or of a solid NATO, or of a new basis for U.S.-Soviet relations, or of a vital commitment in the [Persian] Gulf—we can achieve a great deal.

"But recent history also teaches that when we are divided over tactics—as in Central America—our policy suffers grievously and our national interest does too."

Powell also said during this speech that the executive branch had "an obligation to keep its own house in order. There must be an adherence to law and to the Constitution, and a willingness to consult and deal openly and respectfully with the Congress, taking legislative leaders into its confidence on the most sensitive matters.

"I believe this administration, after the aberration of Iran-Contra, has reestablished and enjoys such a coherent and cooperative process internally."

In May 1988, Powell spoke of peace in the world to a crowd of 1,500 graduates of the College of William and Mary. The National Security Adviser said:

"Peace does not come about just by wishing for it. History also teaches that peace is possible if our strength is wielded in the service of our goals of freedom, progress, and security. With respect to our adversaries, this may indeed turn out to be a time of great opportunity in our relations with the other superpower on earth, the Soviet Union."

General H. Norman
Schwarzkopf

General Colin L. Powell

Major Norman Schwarzkopf helps a wounded Vietnamese paratrooper in 1965.

General Schwarzkopf confers with Saudi Arabian
Lt. General Khalid Bin Sultan, commander of multinational
forces in the Gulf.

General Schwarzkopf and Saudi Arabian King Fahd review the allied troops.

Brenda Schwarzkopf is applauded by First Lady Barbara Bush
and White House Press Secretary Marlin Fitzwater during
the President's State of the Union address.

General Powell
confers with General
John R. Galvin, the
Supreme Allied
Commander–Europe,
while leaving a NATO
meeting.

In 1988, then National Security Advisor Colin Powell talks with reporters about U.S. problems with Panamanian strongman General Manuel Noriega.

General Powell congratulates one of the American soldiers who participated in the American assault on Panama in January of 1990.

General Powell uses a portable satellite telephone uplink to talk with Washington while reviewing the troops in the Gulf.

General Powell and Secretary of Defense Dick Cheney.

Left to right: General Powell, Senator Sam Nunn,
Senator John Warner, Senator Daniel Patrick Moynihan.

General Powell signs an autograph.

11

Powell on African-Americans and the Military

General Colin L. Powell once claimed that the one thing that always got his goat was criticism that blacks would take heavy casualties in any American war on account of their disproportionate representation in the armed forces.

In an interview with *The Washington Post*, he said, "If one of four, roughly one out of five is black, if the whole force accepts casualties, what would you wish me to do? Move the blacks from the positions they're in so that they will have a lower percentage of casualties? Every part of the force, whether it's Hispanic Americans, Pacific Americans, or lower-income white soldiers, will probably sustain casualties in relationship to the percentage that they represent in the overall force.

"What you keep wanting me to say is that this is disproportionate or wrong. I don't think it's disproportionate or wrong. I think it's a choice the American people made when they said have a volunteer army and allow those who want to serve to serve.

"This is not a question to the Chairman of the Joint Chiefs of Staff. This is a question to the American people."

Blacks make up some 20 percent of the military in America, which is 13 percent black. Powell's office said that as of mid-November 1990, 29 percent of the soldiers sent to the Persian

Gulf were black. This is a controversial subject among blacks, according to *The Washington Post* article.

Powell himself is "proud of the fact that African-Americans have seen fit to volunteer to join the armed forces even if it is a higher percentage in the armed forces than their general representation in the population."

He explained that the new recruits sign up for service for the same reasons he did when he was young: "They come in for education. They come in for adventure. They come in to better themselves. They come in to serve a period of time and then get out and use the benefits we have provided them to go to college or get some kind of vocational training."

Ironically enough, before Iraq invaded Kuwait, some blacks were criticizing Powell himself for the planned restructuring and diminishing of the military; they claimed that his work would lessen job opportunities for blacks. Powell figured he could not win no matter what he did—he had a sort of Hobson's choice in perpetuity. There were always going to be critics, like it or not.

"Is it unfair to allow Americans who wish to join the army or the navy, the air force or the marine corps, because that's their choice?" Powell asked.

He answered his own question: "If it were unfair—and I don't accept that—the only way to correct that unfairness would be for somebody to instruct me to set a limit—I won't say quota—on the number of blacks allowed to enlist.

"The armed forces have always provided opportunities for blacks, which blacks have found attractive and have gone after, and I see no reason to change that now."

Regarding the black or white troops that wound up in Saudi Arabia, Powell said that "maybe they didn't want to go to Desert Shield. Nobody wanted to go to Desert Shield and maybe they were hoping that in the time of their service they would not be called. . . . But disappointed as they may be that the prospect [of combat] is here, they understand their obligation. An army exists fundamentally to fight [if *needed*].

"Do they want to come home? You betcha. Do I want to bring them home? You betcha. But there's a job to do right now, and that's what the American people have paid for: a force to be used if necessary, not to just sit around and eat up the taxpayer's dollar.''

Always on the lookout for racism in America, Powell made sure at the Pentagon that there was no racism. He personally made special efforts to encourage young black troops and also kept tabs on black officers who he thought had a bright future in the army.

On August 17, 1989, Powell gave a speech to the National Association of Black Journalists in New York City about the importance of black soldiers in the American army. He said:

''Beginning in the Revolutionary War where one-sixth of those who fought for freedom were black, through the War of 1812 and the Civil War where black men contributed to the freedom and preservation of the Union that we now enjoy, to the buffalo soldiers of the late nineteenth century to San Juan Hill when four black regiments went up that hill with Teddy Roosevelt. We've never seen a picture of them, but four black regiments went up that hill.

''Through World War I and World War II, integration in the late 1940s when the nation finally had to look itself in the mirror and see that you could not ask men to die for a country if the country was not willing to give them their due as full citizens, through Korea, through Vietnam until finally we reached my generation in the military, a generation where almost all barriers have now dropped.

''The generation that saw Chappy James come along and prove that he was as qualified as anybody to drive an F-4 airplane, or Frank Peterson come along to become the first black marine aviator and fly it like few ever have flown the jet plane, or General Rosco Robinson, who became our first black army four-star [general], and not only demonstrated that he could be a great commander of our All-American 82nd Airborne Division, but who also was senior army officer in Japan and . . . could also serve in NATO as a representative of his President and his country.

''And to General Julius Becktan, who commanded our largest combat formation, and first black officer to command a corps, or General Bernard Randolph, now in the air force, four stars, who commands our Air Force Systems Command, or even Major General Harry Brooks (retired), who started out with me many, many years ago when I was a lieutenant and [he] a captain. I was a lieutenant, he was a captain, and went on to a distinguished career in the military before now moving out to a distinguished career in corporate life.

"And not only these officers demonstrated that we could do it as well as anybody, but so did all those NCOs and soldiers who have served their nation so well.

"So, the real story is that yes, I climbed, and I climbed well, and I climbed hard, and I climbed over the cliff, but always on the backs and the contributions of those who went before. And your challenge, and my challenge is to tell our young people throughout the land, black, white, whatever coloration, that they've got to prepare themselves, they've got to be ready.

"I may have crossed over and climbed the cliff with the help of many others, but now that we are on top of that cliff and looking ahead, there are still more rivers to be crossed, and our young people have to be ready, and now you've heard the rest of the story."

Later in his speech, Powell advocated political agitation:

"And the dreams, great ideas of freedom, human dignity, economic prosperity, have struck the fancy of much of the globe. And the great idea of Frederick Douglas, that if you want the dream to come true, you have to be prepared to agitate, has sparked Estonians and Ukrainians and coal miners in Siberia, university students in Beijing as well as every black man and woman in South Africa. The remarkable thing is that these people seem to be pushing the dream, for the most part, in a peaceful way, and not through mass violence. The violence is now coming from the other side.

"Martin Luther King knew the political potency of this peaceful pursuit of the dream. Indeed, it motivated his very life. But the enormous successes being scored almost daily throughout the world belie the danger that still remains.

"As a soldier, it's the danger in the world that concerns me. It's the danger that I am charged to watch out for, to keep a careful eye on. It's that danger that over one million soldiers that I now command in my current job must always be ready to contend with, and it's that danger that I need your help to combat and to vent and to defend against.''

Powell then went on to quote Martin Luther King, Jr., his hero: ''And the quotation says, 'Freedom has always been an expensive thing,' words spoken by a man who knew, words that I look at several times a day every time I go into my conference room.

''Through the years, men and women have paid a precious price for freedom. Dr. King went to jail for it, he marched for it, he died for it. Lech Walesa went to jail for it. And as we are here today, he may well be appointed prime minister of his country. Nelson Mandela went to jail for it and, tragically, is still in jail today.''

Powell once compared the Persian Gulf War to the Vietnam War when he spoke to a conference of the Veterans of Foreign Wars.

''I make this pledge: in this war, it won't be over until we get a full and immediate accounting of all our POWs and MIAs.'' After the Vietnam War, some 2,400 American soldiers remained unaccounted for—many of them black.

''Iraq is somewhat unique in terms of its ability to threaten and subdue its neighbors, as we have seen with their invasion of Kuwait. I think one of the challenges for us in the future is to make sure that no other small regime accumulates that kind of military power. How to do that is another matter. I don't know. It certainly should be one of our long-term objectives.'' Just as equality of color and race should be a long-term objective.

For Powell's money, the American conflict with Iraq was ''not between Christians and Moslems, it's not between East and West, and it's not about cheap gas. Saddam Hussein says it's between the haves and the have-nots. He's right. He has Kuwait, he stole it, and the world community rightfully insists that he give it back. That's what this conflict is all about, pure and simple: between what is moral and what is immoral, between what is right and what is wrong.''

Powell had always had strong feelings about what kind of a military force he would like the U.S. to have. When eventually he did at length become the Chairman of the Joint Chiefs of Staff, he explained what that type of force would be. He said he wanted it to be divided into four separate forces: "heavy," "lighter," "contingency," and "strategic" forces.

A heavy force would be capable of fighting a medium- to high-intensity battle and would be kitted with tactical nuclear weapons.

A lighter force would be used to defend U.S. troops and ordnance in Korea and Hawaii and in other Pacific areas that have U.S. interests.

A contingency force would be able to deploy rapidly from the U.S. into troubled areas such as Panama or Grenada.

Last, a strategic force would consist of nuclear weapons in order to stave off a superpower confrontation.

He then went on to say that he wanted to be more open with the Soviets, even though he was at loggerheads with other members of the Pentagon regarding his approach, which many thought "unique." He did not want to confront the Soviets as enemies—"I want to deal straight up with them as businessmen . . . like two real estate lawyers closing a deal. I want title insurance, I want a termite inspector."

He explained, "The problem we have is everybody wearing a uniform now has spent from the last one year . . . to the last thirty-five years thinking about this in a different context."

Above all else, he told a hearing of the Defense Subcommittee of the House Appropriations Committee on February 8, 1990, the U.S. military needs "most of all . . . a quality force consisting of quality people who are proud to serve in uniform and whom the American people are proud of. It took us ten years to rebuild that after what we went through in the seventies.

"You all remember the hollow army, hollow navy, hollow air force, hollow marine corps. I commanded hollow units when I was a lieutenant colonel and a colonel. I am now the Chairman of the Joint Chiefs of Staff and I am not going to preside, if there is anything I can do about it, over a return to that kind of hollowness.

"The Secretary [Dick Cheney] and I have had many conversations about this subject, and the kind of force that we ultimately will have is a function of how much the American people are willing to pay for that force and the level of risk they wish to see associated with our force posture.

"Whatever that dollar amount is, whatever the American people and the Congress, the administration come to a conclusion on, we will take the force down to match that number so that when we are at that new strength level, the strength level we are at will be a good force, a quality force, a trained force, a ready force, a force that can perform a mission and not just sit around painting rocks, no more going back to the pre-World War II days of Schofield Barracks of *From Here to Eternity*. It'll be a good force and that's the kind of force the American people deserve."

Elsewhere he once said of the military:

"We need to have an honest debate with the Congress and the public about the exact size and shape of our armed forces. Discussions about the number and mix of our forward deployed forces, the balance of active, reserve, and mobilizable forces, and the type of mobility forces required, are valid subjects for debate.

"But we cannot arbitrarily jump from today's headlines to a major cut. We must include all of the other factors in our analysis: remaining Soviet military capabilities, progress in arms control negotiations, economic developments, our enduring national interests and objectives, domestic developments, and above all for the military, a coherent military strategy which coincides with the national strategy."

Powell calls racism "the struggle." He claims that "institutional racism" sabotaged the careers of black officers who were given "dead-end assignments" in the army before he joined it. Powell's career, he has admitted, was "helped by the sacrifices of a lot of great guys who went before me, who led the charge, but did not benefit from the results of that work."

Perhaps when Powell was jumped up over a number of senior generals to the office of Chairman of the Joint Chiefs of Staff, none of the said generals complained publicly because they did not want to open themselves up to charges of racism, a charge that could lay waste to their careers in this day and age.

In fact, *Ebony Magazine*'s Laura B. Randolph has already

leveled charges of "exclusive whiteness" at the man in charge of U.S. foreign policy and national defense.

Emphasizing Powell's blackness, Randolph wrote: "For what we have here is an unprecedented case of the nation's official power structure respecting a black man so much that it is willing to welcome him into the ultra-exclusive club of global power and to rely on his judgment about the safety and future of the nation."

For his part, Powell prefers hands down the black media to any other media. After he was appointed as Chairman of the Joint Chiefs, he picked *Ebony* as the first publication to interview him.

"I have always tilted toward the black media. I've made myself very accessible to the black press and I do that as a way of showing people, 'Hey, look at that dude. He came out of the South Bronx. If he got out, why can't I?' "

Powell never dwelt on his color. He attributed his success to hard work. In Horatio Alger-like words, he once wrote, "There are no secrets to success; don't waste time looking for them. Success is the result of perfection, hard work, learning from failure, loyalty to those for whom you work, and persistence. You must be ready for opportunity when it comes."

In spite of his own personal accomplishments in the military, Powell is probably most proud of his work in the war against racism. In 1988 he told the Joint Center for Political Studies, a black think tank in Washington, DC, that he would never forget the blacks who "suffered and sacrificed to create the conditions and set the stage for me. And I am also mindful that the struggle [against racism] is not over . . . until every American is able to find his or her own place in our society, limited only by his or her own ability and his or her own dream."

12

General Powell: Chairman of the Joint Chiefs

After George Bush won the presidential election in 1988, he summoned General Colin L. Powell to his office and sat him down.

"I think I ought to have my own National Security Adviser," he told him flat out.

Thus ended Powell's service in that post.

It was a sad day for Powell, a bad turn, a painful blow. He was crushed. Of course, it was almost a foregone conclusion, still . . .

"I went home to watch the inauguration on TV," Powell recalled. "At one-thirty that afternoon I absentmindedly picked up my White House phone to place a call. It was dead."

Powell was in a quandary. What should he do next? What would be his next assignment?

General Carl Vuono, the army chief of staff, phoned Powell and said, "If you want to come home to the army, we have a job for you." Almost simultaneously a New York agent informed Powell that he could make oodles of money by getting himself on the lecture circuit.

Powell decided to make a list of options in order to consider in what direction he wanted to go. He drew up two columns on a leaf of paper, one labeled "Reasons to stay in the army" and the other, "Reasons to leave the army." A dozen reasons came to mind to stay.

"But when I got to reasons to leave, I had only one. Money."

The choice was simple. He received his fourth star and assumed control of the army's biggest single command force, the Forces Command, at Fort McPherson in Atlanta, Georgia.

Here Powell had to guarantee that one million-odd active-duty army soldiers, national guardsmen, and reservists would always be on call prepared to defend the United States, and be ready to go wherever war broke out around the world.

A reporter once told Powell he was a lucky duck to escape the Harlem ghetto. Before answering, Powell pondered for a while and then said, "Having my pictures show up in *Army Times* at a critical moment was luck. Finishing Number Two at Leavenworth was hard work. Hard work generates good luck—and opportunities."

Whether it was luck or hard work or a combination of both, President Bush made his final decision on who would become the Chairman of the Joint Chiefs of Staff on August 10, 1989. The man with the appointment would be Colin L. Powell. In accepting the appointment, Powell became the first black man and the youngest man to fill the post. He was fifty-two years old at the time, and, of course, a four-star general.

Of Powell, Bush said he "will bring leadership, insight, and wisdom to our efforts to keep our military strong and ready." Bush went on: "It is most important that the chairman . . . be a person of breadth, judgment, experience, and total integrity. Colin Powell has all those qualities and more."

Bush added that Powell was a man with a "truly distinguished military career" and a background as a "distinguished scholar," who would have a "significant role in determining our military requirements and in developing the defense budget. He is the principal adviser on all military issues to the Secretary of Defense and to [me]."

Powell's response: "Mr. President, I am ready to go to it."

Powell's confirmation was left up to the Senate Armed Services Committee, which was chaired by Sam Nunn (Democrat, Georgia), who called Powell an "excellent nominee" with "proven abilities and experience [that] provide a sound foundation for his advice on wide-ranging defense issues in times of severe budget constraints and a rapidly changing international scene."

Defense Secretary Richard B. Cheney said that Bush expected Powell to serve two two-year terms as the nation's top military adviser.

Brent Scowcroft would become Bush's National Security Adviser. Cheney claimed that there would be no conflict between Scowcroft and Powell on the matter of influencing the President. As Cheney put it, "Their responsibilities are very different. Colin will come to the table as the guy in uniform— the only guy in uniform at the table. Brent certainly understands that; he's been a military officer himself.

"The rest of us sitting around the table are all civilians, and Colin is there to offer military advice. He's not a member of the National Security Council; he's a military adviser. But he has that extra added advantage of having had the same position as Brent is now in."

Cheney predicted that "Colin will be marvelously helpful not only in terms of managing the department but also in strategic arms reduction, conventional arms reduction, chemical weapons," and the parceling out of money to the various military services.

Caspar Weinberger wrote of Powell's qualifications for his new post:

"First, he is a superb soldier whose greatest ambition has been to command troops in the field. He has done that many times, including tours in Vietnam, where he was wounded. But his other talents have attracted presidents and cabinet members whose urgent pleas for his services he has heeded regardless of his own preference.

"Second, he is a great patriot in the best and truest sense of the word. He is not blind to America's faults. He has suffered under them—fighting a war in Vietnam we never intended to win; and his wife and family, while he was away fighting that war, living in the miserable conditions that prevailed in parts of Alabama in the sixties. None of that embittered him nor did anything but convince him that he should fight harder to correct those faults, which he has consistently done.

"Third, he has a truly global, nonparochial view of the world and the leadership role we must play in it. His work as chief military assistant to the Secretary of Defense and as National Security Adviser to the President uniquely qualifies him to know the extent and vital necessity of our commitments, and leaders, civilian and military, with whom he will be working."

Weinberger was impressed with Powell as early as 1972, when Powell was a White House Fellow assigned to work at the Office of Management and Budget, where Weinberger was the director. Carlucci was Weinberger's deputy at the time. They were both impressed with Powell. "He was absolutely tops," Weinberger recalled.

He also met up with Powell in 1980 during the Carter administration when Powell worked for Defense Secretary Harold Brown. Powell was asked to escort Weinberger to the Pentagon when President Reagan assumed office.

One White House aide said, "Powell has many of the qualities that Bush admires. He's a team player, highly capable but modest. And he knows how government works from the inside."

Some commentators saw Bush's choice of Powell as a political salvage job, as it came close upon the heels of the Senate's rejection of William Lucas, another black nominee, as head of the civil rights division of the Justice Department.

For Powell, his new post as Chairman of the Joint Chiefs of Staff was a long way from Harlem. He had never dreamed he would rise to such lofty heights:

"My ambitions, such as they were, were much more modest at the time. They were simply to get out of New York, get a job and go out and have some excitement. At that time I never even thought seriously about staying in the army. My parents expected that, like most young men going in the army, I would serve for two years . . . and then come home and get a *real* job."

Powell maintained he would use his new position to combat racism in America. In an interview with *Ebony Magazine*, he said, "If you check my stats around here you'll find I've been to elementary schools, junior high schools, high schools trying to get the message out every way I can.''

He admitted he was proud of black reaction to him: ''It's been enormously flattering to me to see the reaction from the black community. It's been a source of great pride to walk into a store and have a black young man come up and say, 'I just wanted to shake your hand.' Or to drive through a parking lot . . . and have somebody chase me down to get a signature.''

Powell hoped he could use his powerful position to shape America's policy toward South Africa. He knew, as Chairman of the Joint Chiefs of Staff, that he could not set U.S. policy on South Africa and could not ''get into a dialogue [about] specific actions we should be doing to help specific antiapartheid groups.'' However, he could ''encourage my government . . . and all governments that believe in freedom and democracy . . . to do all they can to bring apartheid to an end.''

In the hierarchy of command, the Chairman of the Joint Chiefs of Staff has no actual legal position. Basically, he commands the American armed forces as a kind of stand-in for the President and the Secretary of Defense. In his post, Powell would serve also as the chief military adviser to the President, as well as the man in charge of figuring out who gets what of the $290 billion military budget. Powell replaced the retiring chairman, Admiral William Crowe, Jr.

As Chairman of the Joint Chiefs of Staff, Powell began right away to use all his political savvy in arguing his case in Congress for a budget of billions of dollars for the Pentagon. He also bent noses out of joint in the Pentagon because the President had jumped him up to his post over some thirty-six generals who had more seniority than he had. Apparently these generals did not know that in politics, political connections were everything. Or, as they say out in Hollywood, virtually a mirror image of Washington, ''It's not what you know, it's who you know.'' Ungrammatical or not, it says it like it is.

These thirty-six generals would all have to console themselves with the fact that President Bush's selection of Powell was a political decision and not one based on seniority. Cold comfort for the slighted thirty-six.

In any case, blacks praised Bush's choice of Powell. Also, Powell had good contacts in Congress, where the Chairman of the Joint Chiefs would have to wage budget battles rather than military ones. Powell also had wide experience in the White House, which no critic could deny.

Powell normally kept his political views to himself, and still does. He is not a registered Republican or Democrat. However, he always goes out of his way to speak out against racism in America, though he believes no new laws are going to change matters.

He once said, "There are no more major civil rights laws to be passed. What we are dealing with now is changing of hearts, changing of perspectives and of minds. We need to start to erase the cultural filter with respect to minorities."

The four-star general put it this way to the National Association of Black Journalists Convention in New York: "[My] appointment would not have been possible without the sacrifices of those black soldiers who served this great nation in war for over two hundred years."

As Chairman of the Joint Chiefs of Staff, Powell has unhesitatingly advocated the use of military force to solve problems. He has shown more willingness to use force than any of his recent predecessors. He believes you should overwhelm the enemy with firepower from the start.

"Don't count on the easy ways," he counseled the President. "You can't put a ship in the [Persian] Gulf and lob shells and do anything. If you finally decide you have to commit military force, you've got to be as massive and decisive as possible. Decide your target, decide your objective, and try to overwhelm it."

He learned these lessons in Vietnam, where the war dragged on for years without any clear objective ever in sight. Americans never launched a massive and decisive assault on North Vietnam. Instead, sporadic battles were levied without a dominant amount of American firepower behind them. In Powell's lights, you must be willing to assert maximum force in a war in order to win it. He would put his theories to the test later during the war with Iraq.

According to one of Powell's friends, "Colin likes to say

that if you want to be a world power, you have to perform like one.''

Before the situation in the Persian Gulf became crucial, Powell had a chance to test out his theories in Panama during Operation Just Cause—the military campaign to oust strongman and alleged drug trafficker Manuel Noriega. Powell recommended to Bush that the U.S. flood Panama with armed forces; he told the President that the military would have to run Panama perhaps for months after they invaded the country.

Powell's views on Noriega had gone in a 180-degree circle in two years. Under President Reagan, Powell had advised *against* using the U.S. military to dislodge the dictator. But the situation had changed.

In a nationally televised press conference on December 20, 1989, Powell promised Americans in his no-nonsense style, ''We will chase him [Noriega] and we will find him.''

His forceful demeanor impressed many. Retired General Daniel Graham, an acquaintance of Powell's for several years, said, ''His performance before the press at the time of the Panama invasion was the best I've ever seen a flag or general officer do in my forty-some years in the military.''

Many blacks, however, opposed the policy of invading Panama. They had opposed Powell before in 1988, when a number of black officials had walked out on Powell while he was delivering a speech to a meeting of the Joint Center for Political Studies, a research organization concerned with public policy issues of interest to blacks. They became irate when Powell claimed that American business firms in South Africa were ''in the forefront of promoting black empowerment.''

Regarding the invasion of Panama, U.S. Representative Ron Dellums, a member of the House Armed Services Committee, voiced his objections:

''Unilateral U.S. military intervention in the internal affairs of our Latin neighbors has been a consistent first recourse, rather than a last resort, in our conduct of hemispheric foreign policy. This . . . has helped sustain tyrannical regimes throughout the region, whether of the left or the right, because of the common denominator of opposition to 'gringo imperialism.' ''

Of course, as has been noted, Powell originally shared the

view that America should not invade Panama. What helped change his mind was the killing of a marine in Panama by Panamanian troops.

Even so, Powell admitted, "I certainly agree that we should not go around saying that we are the world's policeman, but guess who gets called when suddenly someone needs a cop."

Actually, Powell received stinging criticism for not advising Bush to use military force when Panamanians had tried to overthrow Noriega with an inside coup. As a result, the coup failed. Bush and Powell reacted to the objections with Operation Just Cause.

Powell and General Maxwell R. Thurman of the Southern Command spent two months painstakingly devising Operation Just Cause—which was, of course, the invasion of Panama. They ordered 26,000 troops into Central America just to oust Noriega. Powell was cautious about putting the lives of all those men on the line, "but when it's clear we're going to use them, let's use them."

He learned from the "lessons of the past, so we could do things better in the future." From the invasion of Grenada he learned that communications problems existed in interservice operations.

Even though America succeeded in removing Noriega from power and plunked him down in a Miami jail where he would for a long time await trial, Powell had a bitter pill to swallow. He was forced to bow out of the 1990 graduation ceremony at CCNY at which he was to be honored. With faces painted white to stand for the civilians who died in the Panama invasion, CCNY students protested the timing of the award to this prestigious alumnus of the university.

The success of Operation Just Cause bore out Powell's theory that an overwhelming force is better than a force adulterated by bureaucratic compromise and circumspection.

American troops did not capture Noriega in the first hours of the action. At the time, Powell told reporters, "It's a complex city and we're not trying to hold every street corner. We're not attempting to occupy the entire city because we don't have that many troops down there."

Powell asserted to reporters that American deployment of

major forces into Panama's capital would stabilize Panama and persuade Noriega loyalists to give up.

Responding to a question on how long it would take to establish police control of the entire country, Powell said, "How long we have to stay there and how much presence we are going to have to maintain are still open questions. Now we're into audibles." Powell sounded like a coach with his use of the football metaphor. This stylistic device jibes with his image of being a regular guy you could invite over for a beer and pizza to take in a football game on the tube.

He projected this image over TV as well. What with his acclaimed presence, explaining the Panama invasion, he became a household name overnight. *The Wall Street Journal* admired his performance, saying it "left politicians and viewers marveling."

On TV Powell's image is of relaxed forcefulness. He once appeared on *The MacNeil/Lehrer NewsHour*. On TV he had been unflappable. Only once did a TV interviewer get under his skin. That was Charlie Rose on *Nightwatch* when he asked Powell a personal question about his parents. Nonplussed, Powell looked on the verge of tears. Finally, his voice caught, and he said, "Well, Mom, Pop, you brought us up right. All of us. I hope you're happy. I hope you're proud of what we do."

Besides the killing of the marine in Panama by Panamanian troops, Defense Department officials claimed there were four other reasons that changed Powell's mind and convinced him that he should resort to force to oust Noriega.

First, Noriega developed into a symbol of U.S. impotence when Powell was National Security Adviser to Reagan. Nothing the U.S. did got rid of him. The drug indictment against him, covert action against him, and assorted diplomatic attempts against him failed to remove him from power.

Second, as was already mentioned, Powell and Bush did not send the military to help a Panamanian coup that was mounted but failed to remove Noriega. During this coup, Powell did however give authority to American military commanders in Panama to transport Noriega to a U.S. base in Panama if they could do it covertly.

Third, in the eleven weeks after the botched coup d'état, General Maxwell R. Thurman lobbied hard for military intervention in Panama. He asserted that large reinforcements would succeed in driving Noriega from power. He met with Powell several times and pressed hard for military action.

Fourth, Powell had spent much of the time presenting his case for the military budget to Congress. He therefore welcomed the opportunity to show what the U.S. armed forces were capable of doing when Operation Just Cause came along. It gave him a chance to back up his statement to administration circles that "we have to put a shingle outside our door saying, 'Superpower Lives Here,' no matter what the Soviets do, even if they evacuate from Eastern Europe."

Just as Powell's forthright style has always played well on TV, as evidenced by his appearance there to explain Operation Just Cause, this same style certainly went over well with Congress, by all accounts.

At a special Defense briefing regarding the military action in Panama on December 20, 1989, Powell explained clearly what was going on when the U.S. invaded Panama. He did this only seven hours after the onset of the invasion.

For example, Powell said:

"Let me add my own caution that the operation is only seven hours old and it is still ongoing and may be continuing for some time to come. So we're going to give you as much as we possibly can, but please understand that there will be details that I cannot get into for purposes of operational security.

"As you know, at the direction of the President, United States armed forces undertook operations in combat in Panama just prior to 0100 hours this morning, or roughly just before 1 a.m. this morning."

Powell went on. "The participating units include in-place forces in Panama, the 193rd Infantry Brigade, which in recent months has been reinforced by marine units, by a battalion from the 7th Infantry Division at Fort Ord, California, by a mechanized battalion from the 5th Infantry Division at Fort Polk, Louisiana, as well as additional supporting forces to include military police.

"In the course of the evening additional forces have been

added, and I'll describe how they have been added. Those additional forces include a brigade of the 82nd Airborne Division, two Ranger battalions, selected special operating units. All of this, of course, was supported superbly by the United States Air Force and the United States Navy, and there are additional reinforcing units that will assist in stability operations coming from the 7th Infantry Division at Fort Ord, California, as well as from the 16th MP Brigade at Fort Bragg, North Carolina. As you know, our purpose, as stated by the President, is to protect Americans, to protect the integrity of our treaty, to restore democracy in Panama, and bring to justice the fugitive Mr. Noriega.''

Here Powell clearly stated the goals of Operation Just Cause. He then went on to describe in precise terms the military action:

"We conducted operations this morning, beginning just before 1 a.m., in three general areas that General Kelly will point out on the map. First, in the central Panama Canal Zone area, to the east of that, near the International Airfield, and to the west down by Rio Hato.

"Let me now turn to the larger map and discuss each one of these pieces in turn. Let's start up on the Atlantic Caribbean side, with Task Force Atlantic. Task Force Atlantic consisted of a battalion from the 7th Infantry Division and a battalion from the 82nd Airborne Division, which was in the Jungle Operation Training Center in Panama.

"Their mission was to secure several critical sites in the southern portion of Task Force Atlantic AO—the prison at Gamboa, which was secured in the course of the morning and within which there are some PDF personnel who had been put in jail as a result of the coup attempt earlier in the fall, and we now have some forty-eight very happy prisoners who have been released; the electrical distribution center at Sierra Tigre is now secure; and Madden Dam, a critical facility, is also secure.

"Other elements of Task Force Atlantic also ensured the security of our installations in the Colon area, and they neutralized the 8th Infantry Company of the PDF, which did not take too active a role in this operation, as well as neutralizing the naval infantry unit, located up toward the north. There is still some sporadic firing up there. The situation isn't completely resolved, but for the most part, Task Force Atlantic has completed its assigned missions.''

Later in this speech Powell gave a good example of his concise manner of answering questions, which went over well with the audience. Here is part of the Q & A:

Q. Can you—was the resistance from the PDF greater than you expected, less than you expected? Can you characterize how well they have been fighting? How well organized?

A. They resisted. We expected them to resist. There were a number of them quite loyal to General Noriega. They demonstrated that during the coup of October 3. And so we were prepared for that and went down in sufficient force. So, they did resist. They didn't resist for long, because we put sufficient force in the control situation, and for the most part, organized resistance has ended, as the President mentioned a few moments ago, and what we are into now is mopping up and chasing down those who have broken out of the Comandancia or have escaped from Rio Hato and maybe are wandering around Panama with weapons and have not yet decided that it's time to give it up. So we're into stability operations now. For the most part, organized resistance is over.

Powell was not only the youngest Chairman of the Joint Chiefs of Staff but was the only one who never attended West Point or the U.S. Naval Academy at Annapolis. He has always felt equally at home with troops in the field as with members of Congress.

As Joint Chiefs Chair, Powell inherited an office that overlooks a marina on the Potomac River. It has bombproof glass windows. Behind his main desk is an antique shotgun presented to him by Mikhail Gorbachev. On a shelf is a menorah, the seven-candle symbol of Israel. In fact, Powell learned to speak a smidgen of Yiddish, which he picked up while living in Harlem.

Sometimes when he wants to make a point with employees

of the Defense Department, he'll toss Yiddish phrases into his speech. He has become so popular now that you can see his life-size cardboard cutout on the streets of Washington, along with other luminaries such as George Bush, Mikhail Gorbachev, and even pop singers Michael Jackson and Madonna. Tourists line up to stand beside these cutouts and have their pictures taken for five dollars.

As Chairman of the Joint Chiefs, Powell is immensely proud of his family. He said, "In our family, it doesn't make a great deal of difference whether you are Chairman of the Joint Chiefs of Staff or you have a good job as a nurse. We have everything from judges to CEOs to chairmen of the Joint Chiefs of Staff to ambassadors."

As Chairman, he had this advice for young second lieutenants just getting started in an army career:

"Second lieutenants don't even know who the Chairman of the Joint Chiefs of Staff is. Second lieutenants shouldn't worry about being Chairman of the Joint Chiefs of Staff. Second lieutenants should worry about the forty guys they have got responsibility for. Don't worry about graduate school, going to staff college, going to the War College, being a general, or any of that crap. Just take care of your soldiers and have fun. That's what I did.

"I knew who my company commander was, who my battalion commander was. The rest had nothing to do with me. Too many young people stand up there and say, 'Gee. One of these days I'm going to be the chairman, or the chief of staff, or I'm going to be a general.' I tell them, 'Oh, stop all that. Just go do the best you can and stop worrying about it.'"

He encourages them to work hand and foot. "When I talk to young officers now, I try to encourage them to study as hard as they can. Understand military history. And get as much experience as they can in understanding not only the military parts of their career but the political dimensions, the broader dimensions of policy in which national security and military matters operate. If the second lieutenants are anything like I was, a second lieutenant wouldn't be listening to me either. It's kind of like, 'General, get out of here. Tell me when we're going to the training area, or how many bullets will I have for my tank next year.' ''

He added: ''I don't want to leave the impression that they are unthinking young people. They are not. They are far from unthinking. They are very sophisticated. The challenge is to keep them from being too sophisticated at the expense of watching out for their forty soldiers.''

13

General Schwarzkopf:
Once More unto the Breach

After his return to Fort Stewart in 1983 following his successful campaign on the island of Grenada—successful at least from a military and a political point of view—General Schwarzkopf inured himself once again in the work he had been assigned to Fort Stewart to do: run the 24th Infantry Division, which was stationed there.

In a manner of speaking, he had more or less exorcised the syndrome of Vietnam failure by his Caribbean adventure—but there were those who did not agree fully with the military's estimate of the mission. Nevertheless, Schwarzkopf knew that mistakes had been made on the island, and he mentally began to sort out the moves that had worked and the moves that had not.

Most of the glitches had cropped up because the command had lacked proper intelligence information upon which to base moves and countermoves. Such an assessment was common knowledge in the Pentagon. Information had come down to all levels concerning this fact. And this data the general stored in his mind for future use.

Now he was keeping his eye on what was going on in the primary war zone of the world, the Iran-Iraq border. Schwarzkopf studied the battle tactics of the two commands, and shuddered at the implications of the grinding kind of trench warfare that was being waged. Mostly it ground up human flesh—preparing men and boys for burial with monotonous regularity. In no way did this kind of chomping up of bodies resemble traditional modern-day warfare. It seemed something out of the dark and deadly past.

To catch up on Schwarzkopf's military career since he had commanded the 24th Infantry Division (Mechanized) at Fort Stewart, Georgia, and had become involved in the invasion of Grenada in 1983, he was, first of all, transferred from Georgia in 1986 to become Commanding General of the I Corps and Commander of Fort Lewis, Washington.

Then in 1987 the Pentagon called and he was made Deputy Chief of Staff for Operations and Plans, Headquarters, Department of the Army, The Pentagon, Washington, DC.

By now he was a four-star general. In 1988, after two years in Washington, he was assigned to the post of Commander in Chief of the United States Central Command of the Army—called "CentCom" in military jargon. He moved his family down to MacDill Air Force Base in Tampa, Florida.

Central Command was a kind of catchall for countries located in part of Europe and part of the Orient—much of what was now called the "Middle East." Included in the number of countries involved in the military surveillance operated by CentCom was Iraq, lately (1987) just quit of the extended Iran-Iraq war.

Schwarzkopf knew Iran, of course, better than Iraq, since he had been there as a youth and had fallen in love with the life there. Because he had been close to a number of people in Iran, he had the average Iranian's distrust and suspicion of Iraq and the men who ran it. Chief among these was, of course, Saddam Hussein, who had waged the Iran-Iraq war for so very, very long.

As soon as Schwarzkopf was ensconced in Central Command activity at MacDill Air Force Base, he found himself being hectored by forces at the Pentagon to reduce the presence of America in the regions of the Middle East. It was the prevailing opinion of the top brass that by getting out of that area, things could eventually be caused to cool down. This was an opinion not shared by all; nor was it shared by General Schwarzkopf.

The U.S. Navy was already canceling its escort missions for reflagged Kuwaiti tankers in the Persian Gulf. There was also continual effort at the Pentagon to reduce further the number of men in the area. Schwarzkopf did not feel that this move was at all justified. As a result, he reconnoitered the area himself, on his own time, in his own way. He later said he had logged at least three hundred thousand miles flying around the Gulf in his first months in Florida.

The eyes that were focused upon him from Washington did not like what they saw. They knew Schwarzkopf and they knew his record. The fact that he was on his own—well, not really on his own, but at least independently pursuing the kind of eyeball surveillance of the area—made some of them nervous.

Schwarzkopf took it all in stride. On one of his tours in the fall of 1989, he even visited Kuwait. He was worried about the tankers that the U.S. Navy was seemingly abandoning to the forces of the Gulf.

One story had that it was at one of those visits to friends and colleagues in Kuwait that he was invited by the host to garb himself in the traditional dishdasha robe worn by the Kuwaitis in order to be more comfortable in the crowd. He was the only one in a traditional Western suit and tie.

"Holy smokes," the story had Schwarzkopf thinking. "Schwarzkopf is going to dress up like the Kuwaitis and all the Arabs are going to say: 'Who the hell does this guy think he is?'"

Nevertheless, before dinner, he ordered an embroidered dishdasha delivered to his hotel room. There he slipped it on over his body and looked at himself in the mirror—first from one side and then from the other.

He grinned and burst out: "It's wonderful!"

Absolutely overwhelmed by the reflection in the mirror, Schwarzkopf found himself unbelievably waltzing about in the hotel room, doing a little dance step reminiscent of the three-step that T. E. Lawrence—known to history as Lawrence of Arabia—had done in the desert when he took off his army uniform and put on Arab robes before going on to form an alliance of Arabian tribes.

In fact, the story was also attributed to the younger Schwarzkopf who had first visited Iran in 1946—but authenticity is not what is important here. It is the spirit of the thing, the way Schwarzkopf viewed the country and its people.

In all, his visits to the countries in the area gave him a great deal of ammunition to spring on his superiors in the Pentagon, and he reminded them that at every turn things were not quite so quiet as they might think they were in the Gulf. It was best, he said, to keep the American presence visible—highly visible—and to await coming events.

Accordingly, one writer printed the complaint that Schwarzkopf made to him. "Oh, they were saying he had all those forces during the [Iran-Iraq] war, and now he's losing them all and he's fighting."

Back at Central Command Headquarters at MacDill Air Force Base in Florida, Schwarzkopf began to work out possibilities for the Near East. Central was actually a "paper" command, staffing about seven hundred people. It was "paper" because it housed no troops, just basically officers and clerks.

On orders from Washington, Schwarzkopf began going through the files at the base and discovered to his chagrin that most of the stuff contained dated battle scenarios that dealt mostly with the Soviet threat to the Persian Gulf area.

"This stuff is bullshit!" he told anyone who was within hearing distance. He knew that the main threat to U.S. interests and Persian Gulf security was far more likely to come from Iraq than from the Russians. Why had no one programmed any contingency measures to take care of Iraq? The point was, Iraq no longer had Iran to contend with. Iraq was free to do whatever it wanted to do.

While there was not actually a power vacuum in the region, all the countries contiguous to Iraq were militarily unsophisticated and weak, in spite of the modern technology they had purchased from the U.S. and Russia. But Iraq had the fourth largest army in the world—fourth or sixth, depending on how you counted matériel and men. It struck Schwarzkopf that the most dangerous possibility of all would be for Iraq to overrun its neighbors and thus hog a majority of the world's oil resources.

Cleaning out the antiquated war-game scenarios Schwarzkopf found in the files, he began playing with some of his own.

"When we sat down and said, 'What is the worst thing that could happen in this region?' the answer came up: an Iraqi push to capture Saudi oil. They were the largest army in the area—the fourth largest in the whole world—and Saudi Arabia was next door to them, and we had no forces there."

Why an Iraqi push? Almost four hundred miles lay between Baghdad, Saddam Hussein's headquarters, and the Saudi oil fields. But still—

"If I was fighting a rational person," Schwarzkopf said, "I could say, 'They wouldn't attack.' But Saddam is a megalomaniac, a dictator, and a bully—willing to destroy his own world rather than admit he is wrong."

And so it was that—in a fashion that was monstrously ironic, as it later turned out—on July 28, 1990, Schwarzkopf convened half his staff, about 350 people, into the auditorium and told them he wanted to perform a command-post exercise—a "CPX" in military jargon—that was actually a computerized war game.

"We're calling this Internal Look Ninety," Schwarzkopf told his assembled staff. "Ninety for 1990." And then he went on to explain the object of the exercise:

"I want you to draft military plans to protect the Gulf of Persia's oil fields from an attack by Iraq."

That was greeted by silence.

"Oh, and by the way, as far as strategy is concerned, you have to be prepared to protect U.S. regional interests, too."

The staff members nodded and the plan went into the works. When the scenario came out of the computers and was put together as a military stratagem, it included an initial move to subjugate Kuwait, seize those oil fields, and consolidate a military position whence to launch a fierce, devastating attack on Saudi Arabia to take all their fields and subjugate the country.

Don't forget, this was July 28, 1990, five days before August 2, 1990—the very day Iraq *did* strike Kuwait, eventually to conquer it. The effect of Iraq's invasion of Kuwait was to put into the hands of Iraq's dictator, Saddam Hussein, one-fifth of the world's supply of oil. If Saudi Arabia were to follow the fate of Kuwait, Hussein would have a stranglehold on a majority of the world's oil supplies.

During the constructing of the war game, Lieutenant General John Yeosock drew his boss aside. Yeosock was enamored of the Patriot missile, and wanted to lobby for it. According to Schwarzkopf's memory, "He deliberately enticed me down to his headquarters, where he captured me and made me sit through a long briefing on Patriot to tell me how important Patriot was to him, and it made sense what he said." Schwarzkopf would not forget the decision he had more or less made even before the *real* war started. Patriot was to be one of the pleasant surprises in the Gulf War.

War games or not, Schwarzkopf's personal life was full of reality. His daughter Jessica was getting ready to start in her first year at the University of Tampa. His daughter Cynthia—sometimes called Cindy—had just received a beautiful fishing rod from him for her birthday.

Then more reality occurred halfway around the world.

Actually, the crisis was fast approaching in the Persian Gulf on August 1, 1990, when Iraq deliberately broke off talks with Kuwait over a border dispute that was reminiscent of the finagling over real estate lines that Adolf Hitler brought up just before overrunning Poland.

Kuwait had lent a great deal of money to Iraq in the war against Iran, and it had not yet been paid back. There was still a lot of uncomfortable competition between the two countries over their oil supplies. And, of course, there was this idiotic map spat.

At 2 a.m. on August 2, 80,000 Iraqi troops of the celebrated Republican Guard moved across the Kuwaiti border and spearheaded south toward Kuwait City, the capital of the country.

The first reports reached Washington, DC, about 6:30 p.m., August 1, Eastern Daylight Time—just as the invasion was occurring.

At 9:15 p.m., Kuwait's Crown Prince and Prime Minister, Sheik Saad Abdullah al-Saban, telephoned the American Embassy in Kuwait City, requesting instant military aid from America to stop the invasion. Sheik Saad requested also that his plea for help not be made public yet; he was afraid that it would be seen in the Arab world as a rebuff to the Arab countries around him.

By 10:30 p.m. Sheik Saad was in the royal limousine heading south to Saudi Arabia with the Emir, the country's leader.

At 5 a.m. Eastern Daylight Time on August 2, the problem was conveyed to President Bush and Brent Scowcroft, the National Security Adviser. Immediately the U.S. froze all Iraqi and Kuwaiti assets in the country.

A meeting of the National Security Council was scheduled for Friday, August 3.

The night before, Schwarzkopf was just getting out of his sweat clothes after a heavy workout, relishing the feel of the hot shower he was about to dive into, when the hot line in his bedroom rang.

It was his old friend and associate General Colin L. Powell, Chairman of the Joint Chiefs of Staff. Schwarzkopf knew Powell, had known him for some time, and liked and respected him.

"Well, they've crossed," Powell said, after getting the usual greetings out of the way. He was referring to the Iraqi troops and Kuwait's border. It was indicative of his reading of Schwarzkopf that he felt no need to do any explaining other than that.

Schwarzkopf shrugged. "I'm not surprised, you know. Now it's going to be interesting to see what they do."

It was in his mind that they were simply staging a dramatic flash in the pan; perhaps they would harass the Kuwaiti oil fields for a day or two, "beat up on the southern oil field," as Schwarzkopf phrased it, and then return to Iraq, having made their point.

But that was not the way it was.

"You'll be here first thing in the morning," Powell said, telling Schwarzkopf of the scheduled NSC meeting.

"Sure," said Schwarzkopf. He knew he was on borrowed

time once again. And here it was only a year from his retirement!

On the plane to Washington in the early hours of the morning, Schwarzkopf looked over the war-game plans in order to have all his ideas in place for the coming meeting.

Within hours he was facing President Bush and the members of the NSC, outlining the plan as his staff and he had drawn it up. There was mention of about 140,000 American troops in the Persian Gulf area. Schwarzkopf watched the faces of those assembled to listen to him.

"Good God, that's a lot of people!" was the expression he read on most of them.

It was only a plan, of course. Kuwait was in Iraqi hands. There was no place to operate from—unless the decks of a few ships in the Gulf. Or, perhaps, the Saudis could be persuaded to *invite* the Americans in. . . .

The President had been in touch with King Fahd, assuring him that the United States would stand by Saudi Arabia, no matter what happened. Later, Bush instructed Secretary of Defense Dick Cheney and Joint Chiefs Chair General Colin L. Powell to brief the Saudi ambassador on the Iraqi threat and on the U.S. troop plan.

On Saturday the meeting reconvened at Camp David, and it was there that Schwarzkopf was able to take those present through the basic scenario of a full plan to move troops to the Gulf and pin back Saddam Hussein's ears.

"This is what it will take to defend Saudi Arabia," Schwarzkopf intoned coolly. Flipping through the charts and explaining each phase of the battle plan, he finally got to the end. He looked around him. The faces were stunned. The numbers now were a great deal larger than they had been the day before. He and Powell had run over things together.

Succinctly, Schwarzkopf said: "And if you want to *liberate* Kuwait, this is what it will take."

From the very beginning this deliberative body, convened to effect a *defense* strategy, was also considering boldly the concept of an *offensive* strategy as well.

In effect, the plan Schwarzkopf showed them on those two mornings was the plan that eventually came to be used in the final execution of the operation five months later—with few deviations.

As Cheney flew to Saudi Arabia to confer with the Saudis about using the area as a staging ground for the defense of Saudi oil fields, Schwarzkopf flew down to Fort Stewart to begin the logistics nightmare that would ensue when he was given the order to begin moving troops into place for action. Then he flew home to Tampa.

Meanwhile, events moved quickly in the Persian Gulf.

AUGUST 4. Iraq set up an occupation government in Kuwait. The European Community imposed a trade embargo on Iraq.

AUGUST 6. The United Nations Security Council ordered a worldwide embargo on trade with Iraq.

AUGUST 7. U.S. combat troops and planes were ordered to deploy to Saudi Arabia. A U.S. Navy task force set sail for the Persian Gulf.

AUGUST 8. Iraq formally declared that Kuwait had ceased to exist. Great Britain joined the rapidly forming multinational force in the Gulf.

AUGUST 9. Iraq closed its borders, trapping thousands of Americans and other Western citizens in Iraq and what used to be Kuwait. U.S. troop strength in the area jumped to 200,000.

AUGUST 10. Twelve of the twenty Arab League states voted to send all-Arab military forces to join the Americans in the defense of Saudi Arabia.

AUGUST 13. Iraqi troops in Kuwait rounded up all American and British visitors from two hotels and transported them to Iraq.

AUGUST 20. Iraq announced that it had moved Western hostages to vital military installations to use them as "human shields."

AUGUST 24. Iraqi forces surrounded nine embassies in Kuwait with troops, including the U.S. mission.

AUGUST 25. The United Nations Security Council approved the use of force to enforce its embargo against Iraq.

AUGUST 28. Saddam Hussein announced that Kuwait had become Iraq's nineteenth "province."

Meanwhile, men and matériel were pouring into Saudi Arabia—had been pouring in almost from the first day Kuwait had been attacked. On August 27, Schwarzkopf arrived at the base he would use as his command post for the following six months. It was not until four days later that he held his first press conference, which, in the event, proved to be a Q & A affair.

"I just want to say that I've had the privilege today of spending the entire day visiting with the troops that are over here in the eastern part of Saudi Arabia," he started off. "I guess what I want to say about that is America is awfully lucky to have the soldiers, sailors, airmen, and marines we have in our armed service. They're totally inspirational. They're proud of what they're doing. They're ready for what they're doing, and they're not complaining about it."

After that the Q & A took over:

Q. How do you assess the prospects for war at this time?

A. When you look at an enemy, you always have to consider two things: number one, his capabilities, and number two, his intent. It's the combination of capabilities and intent that tells you what the enemy is going to do. There's not going to be any war unless the Iraqis attack.

Q. Are you now telling us, then, that there will be no effort on the part of the United States to get [Saddam Hussein] out of Kuwait?

A. My mission here—our mission, the mission of all of us—is very clear. That is, number one, to deter an attack.

Q. [With multinational forces involved here], how are you going to be able to maneuver without getting in each other's way and shooting at each other?

A. You meet with your counterpart commanders. You know where they are on the ground, they know where you are. You work out various SOPS [Standard Operational Procedures] to put into effect in the event various things happen, and that's going on right now on the ground everywhere.

... We're coordinating very closely with them and things are going very well on the ground from what I heard today.

Q. Have you established a chain of command in case [Saddam Hussein] does attack? Who is going to lead the fight?

A. The chain of command on the U.S. side is very clear. It goes from the President of the United States to the Secretary of Defense to the Chairman of the Joint Chiefs of Staff to me to an army component commander, a navy component commander, a marine component commander, an air force component commander, and from there down to the forces involved. On the Saudi side, of course, the chain of command goes from the king to prince sultan, the minister of defense, to General Khalid, who has been put in charge of this operation. General Khalid and I work very closely. We meet several times a day.

Q. Are you assembling a force here that would give the President [the] option to [push the Iraqis out of Kuwait]?

A. The force that I am assembling here is exactly the force that was briefed to the President of the United States that was necessary for the defense of Saudi Arabia.

Q. Do you expect that Europeans and, in particular, the French should intervene more on your side?

A. I would welcome all the help we can get. . . . I'm very pleased so far with the response that we've gotten from some of the European nations.

Q. But do you complain that it's not enough?

A. I am not in the business of complaining. I'm in the business of taking what I've got and making it work.

Q. There are reports . . . that you're . . . weeks away from defending against a ground attack by the Iraqis.

A. If the Iraqis are dumb enough to attack, they are going to pay a terrible price for it. I'm not prepared to state with

100 percent assurance of any outcome at this time. I may be later on.

Q. Surely the United States forces would also take enormous casualties?

A. My job as a military commander is to carry out my mission with the absolute minimum loss of human life on the part of my troops, and that's exactly what I expect to do.

Q. How vulnerable do you think your forces are to a possible terrorist attack?

A. There's no perfect defense against terrorist attacks. The best defense against a terrorist attack is to be ready for it, to do everything you possibly can to make sure that you're alert and prepared.

Q. Since you are unfamiliar to some of us, could you tell us a little bit about yourself, what your priorities are, your principles are? Are you the sort of general who leads your troops up the hill or flattens it with his air force?

A. My goodness! I'm a magnificent leader. How's that? No, I'm just kidding you. I can't answer that question. Now, why don't you ask some of the people that have worked with me in the past and some [that] work with me now. They could give you a much better answer than I could because mine is bound to be biased.

Q. Sir, what has surprised you?

A. I was asked that question the other day. I said, "I'm surprised it's going so well."

Q. Your forces have been told that they are going to defend Saudi Arabia against aggression. . . . Are they going to be told that they're also defending oil which Americans use?

A. No! Absolutely not. . . . What you've got here is a situation where not only is there a mugging, but a rape has occurred . . . an international rape of the first order. . . . I just don't understand why we have to say that the reason why we're doing it is for oil.

Q. Is it true that you failed to accurately analyze the intelligence information you were given about the Iraqi buildup around Kuwait, and failed to predict the invasion when it happened?

A. Are you talking about me personally, or "we"? . . . I would tell you that we knew exactly what the Iraqis were doing. We knew exactly what their dispositions were. And, I think, again, it's this question of capabilities versus intentions. . . . I think it was just a question of they went a lot further than anybody thought that anyone in the world today would go.

Q. How do you characterize the generals in Baghdad?

A. How would I characterize them? I would—this is H. Norman Schwarzkopf's opinion. I think they're a bunch of thugs.

Q. Do you feel more threatened, say over the last week or two?

A. Every day I feel less threatened because every day we are stronger and stronger and stronger.

Q. What is the Iraqi morale?

A. I hope it's lousy. I hope it's really terrible. I hope they're hungry and I hope they're thirsty and I hope they're out of ammunition and I hope they feel very badly about what they did, because they should.

Schwarzkopf's briefing was a rousing affair. He was succinct, he was serious, he was amusing. Not an easy package to market, given the mind-set of most of the journalists involved. Except for a handful of them, he carried the day with the rest because he could field the questions with a minimum of bother and a maximum of good humor.

Wrote Phil Davison for *The Independent* in Britain: " 'Defense' is a word that does not fall easily from the lips of the six foot three inch, eighteen-stone General [Schwarzkopf] no matter how often he repeats that defense, at least so far, is the nature of his mission. His appointment by George Bush was either a strong hint of potential offensive action or simply a message to President Saddam Hussein. In the absence of John Wayne, President Bush could hardly have made his message more plain.''

He went on: ''Asked by journalists in Saudi Arabia what kind of leader he was, the general replied without hesitation: 'I am magnificent.' No one present was quite sure if he was joking.''

The Associated Press's John King wrote: ''When the airmen yelled 'Go get 'em, Gen'rul!' H. Norman Schwarzkopf couldn't resist. 'We'll get 'em all right,' he said. Then he turned quickly to correct himself, mindful of his mission, and the group of reporters trailing him. 'We're going to get them—when they come across the border,' said the commander of the U.S. forces . . . in Saudi Arabia.''

No question about it. Most of them were with him.

14

The Public Powell I

Generally speaking, audiences tend to enjoy General Colin L. Powell's public speeches and press briefings. The celebrity agent in New York who had told Powell that he could make a fortune on the rubber-chicken circuit was not exaggerating.

Though they may be long-winded at times, his talks are always interspersed with humor to liven them up. Powell comes across as a regular stand-up guy—capable of holding even die-hard anti-afterdinner speech advocates.

On October 27, 1988, he addressed the National Press Club in their ballroom in the capital. He started his address out by the usual name-dropping routine.

"I'm still reflecting on a career as spectacular as Al Haig's—before it ends," he said. That got a good laugh. He went on. "If the army hears about that, it might have ended today. I don't know. We'll have to see." More laughs.

Powell explained his job as National Security Adviser at the White House.

"As the National Security Adviser, I don't get out of the White House that often, because I'm always seized with the Crisis of the Day, and my job is essentially to be close to where the President is so we can *deal* with issues that come before the National Security establishment, and so that we can always be *ready* to swing into action the full forces of the United States, and to engage in diplomatic efforts around the world to deal with world events.

"And that almost was the case today, and especially last

night, and it was my concern that I might not be able to be here with you today because of these crises—but, fortunately, the two damned whales are finally gone—''

The audience broke up into laughter; Powell was referring to two whales whose presence too far in from the deep sea had preoccupied the combined resources of the international media for two days.

''And poor Cable Network News will have to find something else to do.''

Again the audience howled.

Make no bones about it: Powell has his serious side as well as his light side. He spoke of peace and freedom at that same luncheon.

''And something else is also going on in the world, not only peace, but a drive for freedom in Burma, in Haiti, in Chile. The people want world democracy. In the Republic of Korea or in the Philippines, people power has already won great victories. In South Africa, the struggle is reaching a new stage. In Latin America, ten years ago, only about a third of the population lived under democratic rule. Today, it's over 90 percent.

''Interestingly, some of the most striking advances toward freedom and self-determination are taking place in the communist world. We see in the Baltic states a powerful quest for self-expression and democracy. In Poland, we see the resurgence of the free labor movement—Solidarity. The government, after years of trying to suppress it, is now forced to negotiate with it. As the Vice President said a few weeks ago, there is still an Iron Curtain, but it's a rusting curtain, and shafts of light are piercing through.''

This was, of course, before the Berlin Wall was breached and before the Iron Curtain could be said to have more or less become obsolete through attrition and inattention.

''Throughout the Soviet empire, the pressures for change are accelerating. Moscow seeks to manage these changes, these pressures, and to challenge them. But it is a certainty that, given the opportunity, people will press to the limits and perhaps even beyond. It's extraordinary; the quest for freedom is turning out to be the most powerful political force in the world today.

"As Americans, we should not be surprised, not if we believe in our own system. But why are all these good things happening now, in this year? Is it blind luck? The policies of the Reagan administration? Gorbachev's new thinking? Or are there some basic trends in the world that are suddenly favorable? I believe that it is a combination of all these factors."

He later said this of peace:

"A so-called peace purchased at the price of surrender is not real peace or security. Clausewitz said that the conqueror always prefers peace in that he much prefers to march into a city unopposed. But such conditions only tempt and invite ingression. In Nicaragua, for example, diplomacy is not doing well, freedom is not winning, democracy is not winning, precisely because effective resistance to tyranny has been undercut and we face the grim prospect of further deterioration and continuing crisis in that suffering country."

At that date, long before the U.S. was at war with Iraq, Powell was pro-Iraq in its war against Iran. Not so surprising for that time, of course, because of America's troubles with Iran—dating from the day the hostages had been taken by the Ayatollah Khomeini.

Powell discussed the Iran-Iraq war then with his sympathy directed toward Iraq. "In the Gulf, Iraq fought back for years with determination to regain the initiative, and Iran discovered the futility of its military offensives, which year after year made no headway and cost millions of lives. It was one of the bloodiest and costliest wars of this century and also posed dangers to this region as a whole and to the oil shipping lanes on which the Free World depended."

Two-odd years later, of course, America would be at war with Iraq. During the speech Powell also stated his views on the Soviet Union and the twin concepts of perestroika and glasnost.

"The Soviet Union has played a constructive role in helping end some of these [international] conflicts, and this must be acknowledged. This has contributed to the overall improvement in U.S.-Soviet relations, which in turn is another of the most important positive trends of the present period. Major changes are taking place inside the Soviet Union and in Soviet foreign policy. And these are related.

"The Soviet leaders are facing up to their internal challenges, and this adds to their incentive to seek a breathing peace in the international environment. Whether this is a temporary phenomenon or a lasting one it is too early to judge. What is clear is that the Soviet leadership does want to concentrate its energies and resources on internal economic reforms.

"It is also becoming clear that the restive nationalities in the Soviet Union and around the Soviet empire taking advantage of the relative liberalization of recent times are going to preoccupy Moscow more than anyone had anticipated. The bold new leadership in the Kremlin has candidly acknowledged the problems the Soviet system faces.

"But the problems are fundamental, even structural. Essentially, perestroika is an acknowledgment of the failure of the Soviet system to provide for its people. Whether it can be fixed as long as it remains a communist one-party system remains to be seen.

"And there is relatively little we can do to effect the Soviet Union's internal evolution. We can continue to press for human rights, as we have; we can encourage steps that are clearly improvements in Soviet internal political practice, even if they do not correspond fully to what we know as democracy; we can lend our moral support to all those decent people in the Soviet Union who seek greater freedom and well-being, and who feel an enormous stake in the survival and success of the present reform program."

In this vein, Powell spoke about the people in a country, as opposed to the government of a country: "As President Reagan likes to put it, 'People don't make wars, governments do.' How governments behave toward their own people is a good index of how they are likely to behave toward other nations. The worldwide trend toward democracy thus offers profound hope."

He put it another way with the following anecdote. "There's a new joke that's going around the NSC and the White House, and it has to do with a question: 'What's the definition of socialism?' Answer: 'The slowest and most painful way to make the transition from capitalism to capitalism.' ''

And he got a laugh on that one, too.

On a more personal level, Powell claimed—somewhat ironically, as it turned out eventually to be—that he had no desire to become the Chairman of the Joint Chiefs of Staff. He had no intention of lobbying for the job.

''I am in active duty in the army and I have made it a point not to go out and campaign for jobs. The only time I did that, I was a young infantry captain, and I lobbied for a job. I lobbied hard. I got it. It was a lousy job. I hated it. I've never done it again.''

At that time, he said, he was content with his job as National Security Adviser, whose purpose it was ''to bring all of that advice [from the Secretary of State, Secretary of Defense, Chairman of the Joint Chiefs of Staff, all of the Service Chiefs] into a coherent presentation of the issue to the President, and to make sure that when the President is called upon to make a decision, he has the benefit of the advice from all of these people mentioned, as well as any person in the administration or in Congress who has a view that the President ought to hear before he makes his decision.

''Somebody has to do that, and that's the job of the National Security Council, the National Security Adviser—to bring all that information together, package it for the President in the most honest, objective, candid way he can so that when [the President] makes a decision, and we then supervise the execution of that decision, I can go to bed at night knowing that the President had the best possible advice upon which to make his judgment.''

As can be observed here, unlike some of Henry Kissinger's more abstruse allocutions, Powell's talks can easily be understood by the public at large, which makes him appear accessible to all the people. That may be one reason that a whole raft of Americans from all walks of life—Representative Jack Kemp, conservative columnist George Will, and liberal actor Ed Asner among them—have begun to think Powell should run for Vice President of the United States.

Somehow Powell managed to *foresee* the success of the United Nations when it came down hard on Iraq after Saddam Hussein had attacked and subjugated Kuwait in 1990, when he told the National Press Club late in 1988:

"And as the UN implements internal reforms of its budget and its administrative practices and as it continues to avoid some of the polarizing General Assembly excesses of the 1970s, there is a prospect, in my judgment, of even greater successes for the organization, fulfilling the promise of its bold and noble charter.

"It has always been recognized that the success or failure of the United Nations depended a lot on the relations between the two superpowers, and as we enter a period of growing cooperation between the superpowers, it is natural to hope that we will see this reflected in future achievements of the UN system."

When asked why the Soviet Union is more open than it used to be, Powell asserted: "The immediate problem they are facing is an economic system that is not up to the demands of the 1990s and the twenty-first century. . . . The Soviet Union is going to get left behind unless they make the necessary investment and . . . make the necessary structural changes to their economy to compete in this environment.

"Now they can have a first-class army, and they continue to make an investment in that first-class army, but . . . unless they wish to use that army for some purpose . . . they have got to turn their attention to their economy. They have got to make a systemic analysis of what's wrong in that society and take action to fix it. And that seems to be clearly what the General Secretary, President Gorbachev, is doing. Now, we should keep our eyes wide open, because in the process of doing this we will always face that question that was just raised: by making that society and that economy more efficient, does it make them more dangerous to us?"

In any case, America must maintain its army, Powell was quick to point out. He made it clear that he has always thought a military career a wise choice for a young person to make.

He repeated his favorite theme: that the army is one of the best careers for a person to pursue. "I would always encourage young people to consider joining one of our services as a way to serve your country. I have been in the army over thirty years—I'm in my thirty-first year—and I've been privileged to serve around the world. I have been through war for two years with American soldiers. People always say, 'Is this the best army you've ever seen?' "

And the answer to that question, he said, came from the heart. "It's always been a great army as far as I'm concerned. The American people have always given us the most wonderful young men and women to serve their nation and give their lives if necessary. The army we have now has got to be one of the best that I've served in in the thirty years that I've been in it. It was with great regret that I came back to Washington at the beginning of last year and gave up working with 72,000 of the finest young men and women this nation has ever volunteered to service."

In fact, Powell thinks the military should be used in the war against drugs. During his speech he said drugs were "a threat to the well-being of a number of our friends—a number of our friends in the world are literally watching their government collapse about them because of drug activities and the work of drug lords. I think the military should be used in that battle, but I think there are limitations on what the military should be used for, and I don't agree with some of the more adventuresome suggestions that the air force should go out and shoot down private planes and that soldiers should be empowered to start arresting people.

"That's not our system of government, and I think that Secretary Carlucci and Secretary Green, and Mr. Taft, and the Chairman are doing everything they can to make a proper contribution to the drug war, but that is not to say there isn't more the military can do, and we continue to find—we continue to seek ways to get the military more involved in what is truly a major national and international problem."

Powell had more to say about the international arena during a speech he gave to the Institute for Foreign Policy Analysis Conference on November 29, 1988. He spoke of the NATO alliance in the following words:

"I want to . . . address my remarks to the importance that

the United States attaches to the [NATO] alliance and will always attach to the alliance. I also want to comment on the nature of the Soviet challenge to the West as I see it, and what I also see as the task for the future.

"Next year we will celebrate the fortieth anniversary of the [NATO] alliance. And the history of the alliance, its challenges, its debates and successes, is well known to all of you. And some of you in this room, as I look around, helped make that history and helped sustain and nurture that alliance by your dedication, by your courage, and by your vision."

Powell had become a past master at deftly stroking his audience to get all his listeners over to his side. It was a skill all politicos needed to promote their careers. Powell used it instead to promote the policies he wanted to succeed.

"Dean Acheson," he went on, "in writing his memoirs, looked back at the tumultuous events of the 1940s and aptly entitled his book *Present at the Creation*. He saw the task facing American statesmen as less formidable than that described in the Book of Genesis, but for him, no less daunting. In Genesis, the task had been to create order out of chaos. For American leaders, Acheson writes, 'It was to create half a world, a free half out of the same material, without blowing the whole to pieces in the process.'

"That wonderful creative period of American history also saw the birth of a new American foreign policy. One that said good-bye forever to the notion of isolationism and accepted the responsibilities of leadership in the West at the dawn of the nuclear era.

"And at its heart was a simple idea, the idea of collective security—the idea that our security should not be purchased at the expense of a fellow ally. The idea that the alliance should be one in which responsibilities and risks were shared, and that idea has become an article of faith shaping the foreign policy of the United States over eight administrations. It has also been the hallmark of the Reagan presidency and I am positive that it will be the touchstone of the Bush administration as well. The simple fact is that the United States will never sacrifice the security of its allies in pursuit of its relations with the Soviet Union."

He then went on to discuss the new Soviet approach to things.

"Perestroika, glasnost, and the new political thinking have entered the lexicon of East-West relations. President Gorbachev has called on us to witness a new creation, one that we are told holds out the possibility of laying to rest our long and enduring struggle. The role of ideology is to be diminished. Decades of Soviet history are to be exposed and then quickly disposed of, labeled as no more than great aberrations to the true intentions of the founding fathers of the Soviet state.

"It is not simply the restructuring of the Soviet Union that we are asked to endorse, it is the restructuring of East-West relations that beckons us as well. How do we respond? Are we witnessing a new creation? And, if so, shall we actively participate in it? Has the phrase 'the Soviet threat' lost all meaning for the West? I think not. . . .

"For us, the challenge will be to build on the positive changes in what remains to date and have the serial relationship, exploring opportunities for progress while keeping in mind the fundamental moral and political divide that still separates us. The divide between East and West is political more than it is geographic. Throughout the past forty years NATO has been confronted by sweeping Soviet diplomatic initiatives designed, we are told, to clear up this divide and ensure a permanent state of peace in Europe.

"Some of them, we discovered, were merely aimed at scoring points with our publics; others were aimed at sowing division between the United States and Europe and even among Europeans themselves. NATO's response has always been to ask two questions: first, how do such proposals advance the principle of our collective security? And second, how do such proposals ease the fundamental sources of tension in Europe?

"And once again, today, the alliance is called on to raise and address these questions. Today it is Gorbachev's call for the construction of a common European home. In this structure, as he proposes it, all nations, East and West, can live in peace and harmony. The Soviets assure us that there would be room in this house for the United States and Canada as well. We appreciate the reassurance, but we did not ask for it, nor do we need it. We are in Europe not at the invitation of the Soviet Union but in alliance with our Western friends.''

Nevertheless, Powell admitted that there would always be disputes among members of the NATO alliance because ''that's the very nature of an alliance of sixteen free nations, and I'm sure some of those disputes have already been discussed here. I like to characterize the alliance as something like a life raft. It never sinks, but your feet are always wet.''

Powell's simile brought an approving ripple of laughter at the sally.

During his White House briefings, he usually indulged in the same kind of somewhat light-hearted banter. Briefing the press on U.S.-Soviet relations on December 2, 1988, he said:

''The question was, does the President have any reflection on how far we've traveled down the road toward improved U.S.-Soviet relationships in recent years? And I think the answer to that is certainly yes, that the President is proud, and has every reason to be proud, of the progress that has been made over the last several years, and I'm sure he will convey that to the General Secretary [Gorbachev]. And I'm sure he will indicate to the General Secretary that what we have accomplished together over the last three years will be built upon by Vice President Bush, and I'm sure that's something that Vice President Bush would endorse.

''I think you all may have seen some of the polling information lately that shows that 85 percent of the American people believe that our relationship with the Soviet Union is excellent at this time and improving. And 11 percent do not, but they haven't heard my speech yet, and so—''

The journalists in attendance at his briefing laughed appreciatively. Powell had a great way with a line. One reporter characterized his image when he delivered a punch line like that as resembling a kind of giant, cuddly teddy bear. Perhaps that was what made his pronouncements go down so smoothly.

It is extremely interesting to note that both generals we are considering here in this book deliberately *liked* to be thought of as bears—not always *teddy* bears, perhaps, but bears nevertheless.

15

The Public Powell II

A dab hand at politics, even though he was never elected by the people to any office, Powell knows how to ingratiate himself with his bosses—i.e., President Reagan and later President Bush—without appearing to suck up to them.

In politics, appearance is everything. Powell never came on all unctuous and flunky-like when speaking to either President Reagan or President Bush. He speaks to a president as though he is merely another person. On the other hand, he has never treated any president with the slightest disrespect. That would be political suicide in Washington. Anywhere, for that matter.

When Powell was National Security Adviser he wore business suits, not his army uniform, and let his staff address him by his first name. On weekends he wore a sport shirt, slacks, and loafers in the White House.

He doesn't get excited easily. On a tense day in February 1987 during the nadir of the Iran-Contra scandal, Powell greeted his new colleagues as they streamed into the Roosevelt Room across from the Oval Office. At the time, Howard H. Baker, Jr., was holding the reins of the White House staff.

"[Powell] was in a sweater," one of the staff recalled. "Very unassuming, but also a presence in himself. You felt reassured that here was a strong hand. It was a steady voice in a room that was filled with tension."

A member of Powell's National Security Council staff once said, "Powell is not trying to be something he isn't. He's a military officer. He's going to go up the hill, straightforward, even though he's going to take some enemy fire. He's not as subtle as some others might be, but he's comfortable with it.''

Powell learned from the Iran-Contra scandal that the government should be careful about what it keeps secret from its constituents. This may in part explain his attempts at being straightforward with people, including the press. It may also explain his attitude toward government secrets. On December 6, 1988, he gave a speech to the Government Services Administration Information Security Oversight Office Symposium in which he had this to say about secrecy in government:

''I very much appreciate the opportunity to speak before such a distinguished audience on a subject of such great importance, because in our system of government perhaps nothing is more difficult than to balance a democracy's need for some secrecy to protect itself in a hostile world and the equally compelling need for an informed public.''

He continued. ''As National Security Adviser and Deputy for the last two years, and in my experience in government, I have fought the problem of leaks and government secrecy and how to balance the needs of an informed public and the needs to protect the public's secrets—not the government's secrets, the public's secrets.

''Before I really get into my prepared remarks, let me get one thing off my chest. Where I have always come out on this issue is that the public interest demands that the government tell the public what the government is doing for the public. That's the way our Founding Fathers set it up.

''The presumption is that an informed public is a more responsible public, will understand what the government is doing, and is in a better position to judge whether it likes what the government is doing, or whether the government should, at some point, be replaced. So, at the same time the presumption is on informing the public, we also have a responsibility to protect the interest of the public by protecting their secrets.

''So it is not government secrets that we bureaucrats husband unto ourselves and do everything possible to keep away from those 'terrible people' in the press who are really not terrible, they are serving the public interest as well, just as the Founding Fathers intended.

"The judgment we have to make is [this]: Are we serving the public interest correctly when we protect public secrets in the name of the public, [and] not in the name of avoiding our own embarrassment, or in the name of trying to shade the facts in ways that are more acceptable to our particular point of view?"

Powell went back into the history books. "In 1777, George Washington instructed one of his subordinate officers as follows: 'The necessity of procuring good intelligence is apparent and need not be further urged. All that remains for me to add is that you keep the whole matter as secret as possible, for upon secrecy success depends in most enterprises of the kind, and for want of it, they are generally defeated.'

"It is fundamental to the continuance of our way of government, our way of life, that our citizens be informed about the workings of their government and to be informed to the maximum extent possible. Nevertheless, as I've already said, the necessity of withholding certain information in the areas of national defense and international affairs has been clearly established. For over two hundred years, democracy and secrecy have coexisted under our constitutional form of government."

He then went on to speak of news leaks that occur in a democratic society.

"Despite its best efforts, the Reagan administration, like its predecessors, did not succeed in curbing unauthorized disclosure of classified information, and I despair after all these years in Washington of anyone ever being able to solve that problem. Some of these disclosures severely undermined our ability to protect aspects of our nation's security.

"And as National Security Adviser, I can tell you the truth of that statement as I see our negotiating positions leaked in public before we have a chance to table them with the Soviets or others that we are in negotiations with, and as I see some of our intelligence sources and methods dry up, because the knowledge of those sources and methods become public information.

"This is not in the public's interest. I have repeatedly emphasized, in my two years at the National Security Council, the dangers of such disclosures. Each link that compromises a secret source or collection method, or betrays an operation or a proposed operation or a bargaining method, may undermine further our intelligence capabilities, and also the willingness of our allies to trust us with their sensitive information."

Obviously Powell doesn't believe every move the government makes should be kept under wraps. He freely admits that the communications media serve an important role in the government. At a luncheon for the Armed Forces Communications and Electronics Association in Washington on October 12, 1988, Powell said the following:

"You would be lost in the West Wing of the White House or anywhere in the senior levels of government these days if you did not have C-Span and CNN to tell you what is happening around the country and around the world. . . .

"Let me show you how these systems tend to merge. I once had a problem having to do with a particular . . . foreign government [for whom] we had some bad news. . . . We had to take a position before the Congress at a hearing that was going to happen at nine o'clock in the morning that was not going to be pleasant news to this foreign country—a very, very close friend. We made the decision at ten minutes to nine to communicate to the Congress our new position.

"My friends at the State Department and in my own NSC staff began to draft cables to go out to that foreign government and let them know what we had to do. That ambassador to that foreign government happened to be at home. He wasn't here in Washington; he was with his head of state.

"We made the notification to Congress. It was seen on C-Span at a hearing at nine o'clock in the morning; and before we could get the cable out of Washington, it had been picked up by a dish in the middle of the desert somewhere in the Middle East. And before we could get the message slugged via some cellular network, I was having my butt ripped by the ambassador to that foreign country nine minutes after it had been announced to the Congress.

"There is an incredible change in the environment in which decision making takes place in Washington. The ability to put a small camera on the shoulder of a single individual, to take him to Dulles Airport, transport him to just about any important place—or not-so-important place but about-to-become-important place—in the world, get images, pictures, and send it back across the entire world, instantly, changes the entire environment in which policy making and decision making is conducted back here in Washington."

Later in this speech, when referring to the time American forces accidentally shot down an Iranian passenger plane on July 3, 1988, he had this to say:

"The key here is [to] get the message out to the American people as fast as you can when you face a situation like this. If there's a lesson I have learned as the National Security Adviser that might be relevant to the audience like this, it is that you have to move information fast and never lose sight of the fact that there are these other environments and other systems out there that are in need of attention, and that if you wish to have a foreign policy, if you wish to convey a story to the world that shows consistency, that shows coherence, then you have to keep in mind the needs of all of these interrelated systems that form one very large and important communications system. And it works. It works rapidly."

Despite his amiability, Powell can also deliver a belligerent speech when he needs to, as he did when he addressed the D.C. Bar Association at the Ramada Renaissance Hotel in Washington on January 10, 1991.

As usual he began his speech with a joke:

"Let me take this opportunity in front of your colleagues to also thank you for the service you've performed for me and for Frank Carlucci when we were all together at the National Security Council in 1987, 1988, and early 1989. I'm delighted I was able to conclude that assignment without ever being indicted, and I thank you for that, sir."

The lawyers chuckled with glee at Powell's droll appraisal of his position in the Iran-Contra scandal.

"And I have been tempted, thinking about today and thinking about Paul's earlier invitations, to foist lawyer jokes on you a bit, but I won't do that. The biggest lawyer joke was foisted on me earlier this year when my son entered Georgetown Law School to become a lawyer.''

More laughter.

But then Powell got down to business as he denounced Iraqi aggression in Kuwait.

''On August second, suddenly and swiftly [Saddam Hussein] invaded Kuwait. The rule of law wrapped itself around his tank treads and snapped and for the Kuwaitis, there was no law at all. On August third Mr. Hussein resurrected the rule of law, twisted it a bit, and announced that certain Kuwaiti leaders had asked him for his assistance, and that he had used military force only at the request of these still unknown and unnamed leaders.

''And on August fifth he announced he would soon withdraw his forces from Kuwait. And then on August eighth he announced that he was annexing Kuwait and that henceforth it would be the nineteenth province of Iraq. Once again, the rule of law lay prostrate under the boot of Saddam Hussein.''

It was fitting and proper that Powell focus his speech on the concept of *law*, fully aware of the fact that he was addressing a group of lawyers about violations of theoretical legality.

''In August and, as you know, in subsequent months, Hussein refused to let foreign nationals depart Iraq, instead using them as 'human shields' to protect Iraqi assets. The rule of law was nowhere in sight, only the law of Saddam Hussein was applied.''

But there was worse to come. ''Mr. Hussein did not perpetrate the rape of Kuwait against the land, the buildings, the streets, the oil derricks, he did it against people, against human beings—men, women, young children, babies. The buildings were not shot in the head, young men and young women were. The land was not stripped of its incubators, babies and hospitals were, and they were left to die. Young men were shot in full view of their families and neighbors, who were forcibly gathered together to watch these horrible executions.''

Powell, indignant now, explained how America intended to fight its war with Iraq:

''Our military concept is simple and direct: put in place a

land, air, and sea capability designed to strike suddenly, decisively, and in sufficient force to resolve the matter alongside our allies; to do it quickly; and to do it with a minimum loss of life.

"Every American life is precious to us. We will exploit Iraqi weaknesses with our strengths. They will not be dealing with fifteen-year-old Iranians being offered up as cannon fodder. They will be dealing with a very powerful, capable force, a force that will have no other aim short of winning and a force with the capability to win."

Powell was asked later what the U.S. would do if Iraq attacked Israel—a touchy question at best.

"That's a very hypothetical question—and, following the advice of my former lawyer, I don't answer hypothetical questions."

The audience of lawyers laughed appreciatively.

Powell tends to answer questions directly whenever he can at speeches and briefings. The following special defense briefing on December 20, 1989, regarded the military action in Panama and the capture of Manuel Noriega.

Q. What assurances do you have that Noriega isn't going to escape into the countryside and organize some kind of guerrilla operations to keep harassing U.S. forces?

A. Oh, he can do that, and we will chase them and we will find him.

Q. Do you know that he's still in the country?

A. No, I don't know that. . . . He is a very canny individual. He's demonstrated incredible ability to survive catastrophe. And we'll see over time whether he survives this catastrophe.

Q. General, now wouldn't he make life miserable for the U.S. forces down there?

A. I doubt it. No. I don't think [so]. It's been some years since General—*Mr.* Noriega, the fugitive—has been seen in the jungle, living in the jungle. He's used to a different kind of life-style, and I'm not quite sure he would be up to being chased around the countryside by Army Rangers, Special Forces, and Light Infantry units of the Joint Operations Training Center. . . . I can't rule that out, but I think that's rather farfetched.

Powell can be evasive as well as sharing, as the following exchange during the same briefing attested:

Q. General Powell, can you explain to us how—why you were unable to apprehend Noriega? The White House said last night that the apprehension of Noriega was one of the objectives of this mission.

A. Yes.

Q. Did you know his whereabouts before you launched this mission? It would seem that you would have. And how did he manage to escape our forces?

A. It's only seven hours into the operation, so I'm not going to get into where we thought he was or wasn't or what we might be doing now. This operation is still young.

Obviously Powell didn't want to tip his hand to Noriega or any of his cronies who might be watching the briefing on TV. That would be tantamount to having a Buffalo Bill in the New York Giants' huddle at the Super Bowl. Who was this reporter anyway? An escapee from *Saturday Night Live*? "General Powell, what's the secret password so we can give it to Noriega?"

During the same briefing Powell showed his sometimes colorful and blunt way of describing things. He said:

"With respect to General Noriega, as you know, we're only seven hours into this operation. We have not yet located the General. He has a habit of changing locations in normal times four or five times a night. But we will continue our efforts to locate him. But, as a practical matter, we have decapitated him from the dictatorship of this country and he is now a fugitive and will be treated as such."

"Decapitated," indeed! This word was a foreshadowing of

one of Powell's most famous quotes concerning the Iraqi army in Kuwait: "Our strategy to go after this army is very, very simple. First we're going to cut it off, and then we're going to kill it."

You can't get much blunter than that.

On the other hand, Powell can sound humble in accord with President Bush's plea for a "gentler and kinder America," as he did at the hearing of the Senate Armed Services Committee on September 20, 1989, for his appointment to the grade of four-star general and reassignment as Chairman of the Joint Chiefs of Staff. Powell addressed Chairman Senator Sam Nunn in this manner:

"Mr. Chairman, I am deeply honored to be here today and humbled to be here today to be the President's nominee to be Chairman of the Joint Chiefs of Staff. If confirmed, I promise to you that I will do my very, very best. As I look at the committee this morning, I see friends. I see senators that I have worked with before—sometimes on the same side of the issue, other times fighting on opposing sides of the issue—but always in the spirit of openness, candor, honesty, fair fighting.

"I promise the members of this committee that I will always approach my dealings with this committee or all of the other appropriate committees and the entire Congress in the same way that I have in the past, because I consider it an article of faith that we both have the same objective, the same purpose, and that is, to see that we take actions with respect to our armed forces that keep them strong, that keep them ready, and that keep us prepared for whatever challenges that may come ahead.

"This is a time of challenge, as the chairman has pointed out. There is anxiety in the world today. There is some instability. People are not quite sure where events are taking us as we see the significant changes that are taking place in the Soviet Union. But as the chairman also said, it is a time of opportunity, it is a time of hope. I think we need to take advantage of the opportunity. We need to respond to the hope that we see in the hearts and minds of people around the world."

That did not mean that Powell was going to be kinder and

gentler toward narco-terrorists. When he was asked at the hearing if it would be appropriate to use U.S. troops to retaliate against narco-terrorists, Powell responded:

"If the retaliation was the type of retaliation that can only be done by U.S. armed forces, such as transporting an armed force to another nation, and if it's done consistent with presidential direction and consistent with our laws, yes.

"Within the United States, there are other agencies that have responsibility for such actions, and I don't think they'd be considered retaliatory actions so much as they would be [considered] law enforcement actions. And, so, I would expect the designated law enforcement agencies of the various states or the federal government to handle that within their capability. I don't see an inconsistency there."

Q. If, in cooperation with and in conjunction with foreign units operating in another country, it was deemed necessary or appropriate to retaliate, do you think it would be appropriate to use U.S. Special Forces, anti-narcotics units, or whatever in actual direct action against drug lords, drug lords' armies, drug operations?

A. If it was beyond the capability of the forces of the country concerned and if they asked for our assistance and if the President so directed, I would have no reservations on that kind of a retaliatory strike. But I don't want to let that answer get extended into the presence of the U.S. armed forces on some kind of regular basis conducting these kinds of operations on a steady-state basis in a foreign country. That's an entirely different question, I believe.

Q. But in special situations?

A. A special surgical retaliatory strike against terrorists who have done something against the United States that the President, within his authority, believes should be retaliated against and after due consultation and consideration the President directs such action, then the United States and armed forces certainly have the capability to conduct such strikes.

Note that Powell did not answer the senator's question. He did not say it would be appropriate to use U.S. Special Forces to attack drug dealers in foreign countries, which was the real force of the question.

All Powell said was that United States armed forces had the "capability" to conduct such strikes. For some reason Powell wanted to dodge this question and he did it skillfully, for the curious senator did not pursue the matter. It is a solid testament to Powell's political skills that he was able to avoid giving a direct answer to the senator's persistent questioning and essentially got away with it.

16

General Schwarzkopf:
The Game's Afoot!

From its beginning shortly after the fall of Kuwait in early August 1990, the buildup of troops and supplies in Saudi Arabia was a logistics nightmare. It swirled around the persona of H. Norman Schwarzkopf every waking moment as well as many of his nonwaking moments.

Once in the desert, Schwarzkopf settled down to a regular working routine that involved about seventeen hours of work a day, allowing him four hours for sleep and rest and another three hours to eat and (perhaps) relax.

His hosts in Saudi Arabia had offered him a special villa for his own comfort, but Schwarzkopf was not a general of that kind. Instead, The Bear chose to make his living quarters in a small room just behind his office space—which was in a huge compound constructed four floors below ground level under the Saudi Arabian Ministry of Defense "somewhere in Riyadh."

"This is home and I drag my body out at seven in the morning and go back in there and start work again."

And work there was aplenty.

For not only was Schwarzkopf kept busy from morning till night in moving people and matériels around on a global basis, but he was gathering together a staff of people who would be working with him when the delicate business of actually running the war began. And most of these men were as involved and as committed to the military aim as Schwarzkopf himself.

One of them, Lieutenant General Charles Horner, who became air force commander for CentCom shortly before the move to Saudi Arabia, explained the logistics nightmare that prevailed around Desert Shield headquarters.

"[It] was like shoveling manure. As fast as it comes off, you push it around."

The six key American figures working directly with Schwarzkopf on a day-and-night basis were all well known to him and were used to working with him. They controlled the five armed services of the United States: the ground, the air force, the navy, the marines, the supplies (logistics). The sixth was Schwarzkopf's chief of staff.

In many ways these men were ideal selections for his immediate staff. Their experience in military operations was profound, and their mind-set was not foreign to that of their tough-minded, no-nonsense commander.

Let's look at them more closely, one by one.

GROUND COMMANDER
LIEUTENANT GENERAL JOHN J. YEOSOCK

"There ain't nothin' pretty 'bout John Yeosock," one of his close friends, also a three-star general, once said. The way it was said was a compliment, not a derogation. Yeosock came up the hard way, and the way he came up was a testament to his grit and determination. Unable to pass the physical at West Point because of poor eyesight, he joined the ROTC at Pennsylvania State University.

A tall, lean man with a lined face, Yeosock came from the gritty coal country in Pennsylvania. After he had graduated from Penn State, he joined the army, and it was there that he found his true avocation. He became enamored of armor—the tanks that were essential to twentieth-century warfare.

He spent a great deal of his time in the 3rd Cavalry. The word "cavalry" is a misnomer for the modern cavalry unit; there are no more horses in war, except for parades and cosmetics. Cavalry now means tanks. And it was tanks that fascinated Yeosock.

Tank platoons were beginning to operate differently from the frontal attack that was used by them in World War II. "When tank platoons attack, they spread out to present a more difficult target to the enemy," Yeosock pointed out. But when they were so widely spread out that they had to operate—in a sense—independently, each must understand the commander's intent, but must use its own initiative.

"The cavalry is not a branch. It's an attitude."

Under Yeosock's command were 280,000 U.S. Army troops. He was in charge of the planning and implementation of their tactics, their feeding, fueling, munitions, movement, support of other forces, medical and maintenance programs, schemes of maneuver, targeting intelligence and other support.

"[It's a] continuous balancing and rebalancing," he said, to make sure that the massive flow moved smoothly along. Yeosock compared it to "running a corporation with one-quarter or one-third of a billion people."

Yeosock's group was moving scores of millions of gallons of fuel—figuring at least 200 five-thousand-gallon tankers to move a million gallons of fuel. "And [for us] a million gallons is a small number."

Yeosock worked a good sixteen to seventeen hours a day, just like his boss, Schwarzkopf, to keep things moving on the ground.

"My predecessor in the 3rd Army, George Patton, in the movie, rode around in a jeep with binoculars. I can't do that. I have to see the picture in its totality. It's a little bit different from Hollywood."

MARINE COMMANDER
LIEUTENANT GENERAL WALTER BOOMER

Walter Boomer came from North Carolina and grew up to be an introspective, very soft-spoken man, whose roots in North Carolina were evident in the slow drawl in which he spoke. "Marines are a lot smarter than you think," he would keep telling people.

Boomer learned about military service in Vietnam, where he served two tours of duty, first as a company commander in 1966–1967, and four years later as an adviser to the Vietnamese marines.

"We made a lot of stupid mistakes in Vietnam, mistakes we're not going to repeat here." Boomer, unlike his boss, H. Norman Schwarzkopf, who blamed politicians and bureaucrats for the bungling endemic in Vietnam, focused his criticism on the military itself. He felt that the policy of rotating officers every six months so that more officers could get combat commands deprived troops of experienced leaders. In fact, he said, it bordered on the immoral.

Boomer's battalion in Vietnam was overrun by the North Vietnamese at one point. Almost half of its number were killed in the Easter Offensive in 1972. Ever since that debacle, Boomer determined that he would hold down the number of casualties in any future conflict to which he was assigned.

As marine commander, Boomer had a seat at the CentCom planning table in Riyadh, but he preferred to run things from the actual field of battle. To keep in touch with command headquarters, he used an aide—a two-star general—to represent him. He planned to keep in constant touch with the aide by calling him at least four times a day. He would call in to Schwarzkopf at least once a day.

"If the decision is not one I like, I'll call [Schwarzkopf]. But sometimes I just pick up the phone to cheer him up."

The marines, of course, were being saved for the ground war, which would follow the softening up by the air war—if such a second phase was to prove necessary. That is, of course, unless Saddam Hussein suddenly regained his sanity and decided to call off the war by default.

AIR FORCE COMMANDER
LIEUTENANT GENERAL CHARLES HORNER

When Charles Horner was once asked to describe himself, he quipped: "I'm a man with absolutely no personality." Every bit of his personality contradicted that image. He was in fact typical of the kind of fly-boy idolized back in the days of World

War II—cocky, happy-go-lucky, and smiling in the teeth of sure disaster.

Schwarzkopf once called him "a superb fighter pilot with a great sense of when to have fun and when to get the job done."

Horner was born in Iowa and graduated from the University of Iowa. He had always wanted to fly jet airplanes, but never had the money to pay for lessons. He enrolled in the ROTC at Ames and that finally got him into the air force after his graduation. He attended flight school, flying forty-eight combat missions in F-105s over Vietnam, seventy more in a Wild Weasel, in which he attacked enemy surface-to-air missile sites in North Vietnam.

He worked his way up in the air force until he became commander of the force in Saudi Arabia. Under his leadership were some 1,800 U.S. warplanes and 435 Saudi, Kuwaiti, British, Italian, and French planes also in the theater.

His daily stint included attending a meeting at CentCom headquarters. Because his air campaign was so closely linked to what was happening on the ground, he stayed in closest touch with General Yeosock, an old personal friend, who was also his roommate in Saudi Arabia.

"Sometimes there are difficulties working with different commanders," Horner said, "but that is not so here. . . . There are no prima donnas among us." He emphasized that the members of the general staff did not spend much time talking to one another. Everything they did was run according to "the campaign plan." In essence, what he was saying was that the schedule itself ran the war.

It was on August 3, 1990, that Horner, then commander of the 9th Air Force, which included all the fighter bases east of the Mississippi, was flying an F-16 to Langley Air Force Base in Virginia when he received a call telling him to return to Shaw Air Force Base in South Carolina.

From there he was called to CentCom headquarters at MacDill Air Force Base in Florida.

From there he went to Washington with General Schwarzkopf to brief President Bush.

Shortly after that he accompanied Schwarzkopf to Saudi Arabia—packed for a few days' stay. Instead of a short mission, he was anchored there for the duration of the emergency, with no respite for him until the end of the war.

NAVY COMMANDER
VICE ADMIRAL STANLEY ARTHUR

In a way, Stanley Arthur was an anomaly in the navy, at least as commander of its forces in the Persian Gulf. He had always been essentially a flyer, rather than a sailor. Nevertheless, he was certainly the right man in the right place when the Iraqis overthrew Kuwait.

Arthur had five hundred combat missions in Vietnam, and won the Distinguished Flying Cross. His command of NavCent was relatively new. He was the last commander to join Operation Desert Shield, being placed in command at NavCent in December 1990, while the forces were being consolidated in the desert.

"He wasn't just in the neighborhood," explained Colonel Frank Wickersham III, the marine liaison officer for the admiral. "And it wasn't a one-shot deal."

The admiral analyzed the overall plans for the softening of Iraq as essentially an air mission, and thus understood that his presence there would add a great deal of punch to the navy's parallel air power, as well as the air force's.

Arthur was put in charge of 120 American ships, including six aircraft carriers, and was responsible for coordinating with fifty more ships and eighteen allied navies. American forces on the sea were scattered about the Persian Gulf, the Red Sea, and the north Arabian Sea.

On his deck on the USS *Blue Ridge*, an elegant, high-tech command-and-control ship that was Arthur's office and home in the Persian Gulf, he kept a hand-lettered sign that read "TMMP."

"That stands for Too Many Moving Parts . . . and that's what I have here!"

Arthur confessed that his main concern was what he called "target deconfliction." That unwieldy mouthful of syllables simply meant that he must pay a great deal of attention to make sure the various air forces sent out to pound Iraq and Kuwait didn't end up running into each other, bombing the same target.

"It's one of the growing pains of the operation," he said. A parallel problem would face him on the sea as well—to make sure that his many navies did not run into one another during the combat to come.

LOGISTICS
MAJOR GENERAL WILLIAM "GUS" PAGONIS

Gus Pagonis was one of the first to be selected by H. Norman Schwarzkopf for the Persian Gulf command operation—then titled Operation Desert Shield. From the beginning Schwarzkopf knew that the basic problem that he and his staff had to face was that of logistics.

For every amateur student of military tactics knew that World War II might easily have been brought to an earlier conclusion if the gasoline had been available for Patton's tank army that succeeded so magnificently that it outran its own supplies of fuel and stalled ignominiously on the way to certain victory.

Other nightmares continued to becloud the services during World War II. "The Germans would attack and take ground and then have to go back and resupply. When they would go back, the Brits would move forward," Pagonis recalled.

Pagonis spent two years as an officer in Vietnam and stayed in the army afterwards, to find himself on call when Schwarzkopf needed him in August 1990. When he arrived in those first days of August, he had a five-man team with him. They worked out of the back of a four-door sedan.

"When we first arrived we were inundated with trucks and tanks and ammunition," said Colonel James Ireland. Pagonis told them if they didn't build a latrine for the troops they were going to lose more soldiers to disease than to battle. "It was his first priority," Ireland added.

His second priority was to get some real American food to the troops. "Right away he set up a mess tent serving hamburgers, chicken, and pizza. Now he's got trucks all over the country doing the same."

Along with meals, he was also responsible for moving in

millions of gallons of water, pumping in millions of gallons of fuel, and distributing 236,300 tons of ammunition to the troops.

And then there were always the live soldiers, too. Hundreds of thousands of U.S. troops!

And Pagonis's work would never be done—or even half finished. When the ground war was ready to go, Pagonis would have to be there, moving men, weapons, and supplies to the front. But he had a plan. He would build six truck stops along the main supply routes—for quick food!

"When you drive at home, where do you stop to eat? Where the trucks eat, right? So that's what [we're going to build]. Get a hamburger, use the latrine, and get right back on the road."

CHIEF OF STAFF
MAJOR GENERAL ROBERT B. JOHNSTON

Robert Johnston once said that he joined the U.S. Marine Corps more out of a sense of duty than any other consideration. Actually, Johnston was born in Scotland, and grew up there. It was not until he was eighteen years old that his family moved to the United States, in 1956.

Johnston was naturalized five years later. When he did become a U.S. citizen, he pledged himself as a new citizen to serve his country. Taking the vow more than seriously, he joined the marine corps for a three-year hitch.

He never looked back on civilian life.

"It seemed that I had a lot in common with marines," he said.

He had been chief of staff at CentCom for only two months when he got a call from CentCom's overall head—General H. Norman Schwarzkopf—to move out CentCom and its forces to Saudi Arabia in toto.

"My God!" Johnston said to himself. "How do we start doing this?"

There was no time to answer that question, any more than there was time to ask other collateral questions that needed asking. Johnston simply started *doing* rather than *talking* and achieved the near impossible.

Setting up CentCom in Saudi Arabia required the transfer of its entire staff of seven hundred people—plus all the matériel at MacDill Air Force Base in Tampa. It was Johnston who with several close aides first arrived in Saudi Arabia, setting up temporary commands anywhere they could—hotel rooms, rented apartments, perhaps an occasional private home.

Now Schwarzkopf's savvy came into play. He had never been utterly sanguine about security from terrorist attacks. It was his fondest hope to get away from rooms and offices and hotels and find a place where his staff could function out of danger.

For a while Desert Shield operated out of an abandoned schoolhouse, and rooms in several Saudi government buildings. But eventually the CentCom staff worked their way down into the ground and set up the elaborate headquarters four stories below the Saudi Arabian Ministry of Defense that served them as their War Room all the way through the action phases of the war.

"I don't get out much," Johnston said. "My job requires me to be in this building more than any other staff officer."

He missed his old life-style in the States. There he used to run three miles and do pull-ups and sit-ups six days a week to keep in shape. He was only able to jog once a week, if that, in Riyadh.

His main job was to manage the structure that provided the information and analysis to operate Desert Storm.

"I like things to be exact. And I have a personal commitment to missions."

In addition to that, one of the first soldiers to arrive in Saudi Arabia after the big lift began was his son, a junior officer in a marine infantry battalion.

"It makes the ground-offensive operation a lot more personal," he said.

It was in the scenario of Operation Desert Storm to move more than a half-million men into battle against the Iraqi forces.

Most of these men were American, but large numbers of them came from separate commands from all over the globe.

Next to the Americans, the British supplied the most troops and matériel from one specific country.

Schwarzkopf kept in daily contact with the three men in charge of the British troops, one of whom was in overall command of the men from Great Britain.

COMMANDER OF THE BRITISH FORCES IN THE PERSIAN GULF LIEUTENANT GENERAL SIR PETER DE LA BILLIERE

Sir Peter de la Billiere liaised daily with Schwarzkopf, working closely with the other commanders of the British troops involved in the war. His two closest associates were Air Chief Marshal Sir Patrick Hine, who was the Commander in Charge of the United Kingdom Air Force, and Air Vice Marshal Bill Wrattan, the United Kingdom Deputy Commander/Royal Air Force.

The British were skilled in desert warfare, had been for generations. The famed ''Desert Rats'' of World War II were no more, of course, but a modern counterpart, the 7th Armored Brigade, was present under the command of Brigadier General Patrick Cordingley. With the 7th was the 1st British Armored Division under the command of Major General Rupert Smith.

There seemed little fear that the British and Americans could work together, even though historically in World War II there had been some conflict at times between the top generals of the two countries.

By the end of December there were about 35,000 ground forces in the Gulf area directly from Great Britain. The force consisted of a large division with two armored brigades, an artillery brigade, engineers, logistics, helicopters, and air defense (antiaircraft, or ''ack-ack'') regiments.

In numbers, the British supplied a number that was two-thirds of the fighting strength that had fought in the British Army of the Rhine in World War II! The 7th Armored Brigade was then enlarged to a division on the advice of Commander Sir Peter de la Billiere.

"A brigade is a relatively small unit and it would have had to follow American thinking and tactics," said de la Billiere. "Being much larger, the division gives much broader direction to allow British equipment, tactics, leadership, and imagination to be used to their best advantage."

Schwarzkopf of course concurred completely, always being a man to cut through the fluff and get right to the action.

The division would act independently, controlled only by the Americans at corps level, and by General Schwarzkopf, the overall commander. When the 7th arrived, it was assumed to be part of the 1st Division of the U.S. Marine Expeditionary Force. Later on, in practice, the reverse became the fait accompli.

Schwarzkopf decided that the brigade would provide the heavily armored punch for the large U.S. Marine Corps. He and de la Billiere cut a deal at the very beginning by agreeing to use British officers on their staff to man planning units at all levels.

The Anglo-American units added up to 450,000 men—the biggest British logistics exercise since the Korean War forty years before.

"It is a long wait in a sensitive and difficult time," said de la Billiere. "None of us can predict the outcome. Naturally, we hope for a peaceful outcome, but this does not mean we are not prepared to fight if we are called on."

De la Billiere's philosophy of military endeavor was not dissimilar to that of Schwarzkopf's.

"Leadership is about taking the men through the ups and downs of waiting—keeping them happy and motivated," he said. "I believe that is what leadership is really about—not being the gung-ho sort of guy who leads his men into battle unprepared, which could bring disaster. I am not that kind of person."

Schwarzkopf's main command problems seemed to stem from the presence of the Saudi Arabian contingent, in conjunction with various Arab states that were fighting side by side with Saudi Arabia. The problem was that they might feel that they should be running the war rather than the Americans.

It was up to Schwarzkopf to work out the wrinkles. One man was crucial in this undertaking.

COMMANDER IN CHIEF OF THE SAUDI ARABIAN FORCES PRINCE GENERAL KHALID BIN SULTAN

Prince Khalid, who could speak fluent English, acted as a proper host to his most distinguished guest, General Schwarzkopf. Khalid was in charge of not only the Saudi Arabian forces but also the troops from Syria, which was a country not entirely happy with any hint of U.S. domination in any area.

There were also troops from Egypt, Pakistan, Morocco, and Bangladesh, as well as others from France and Italy, Greece, the Netherlands, West Germany, Spain, Denmark, Norway, Portugal, Belgium, Australia, Canada, and other countries.

Khalid bin Sultan once said that he and Schwarzkopf would always get along well because they thought alike.

"What happens if you disagree?" a television commentator asked Khalid.

"I can assure you, we will never disagree."

It would be Schwarzkopf who made the decisions and Khalid who agreed—and as it worked out during the heat of the battle that was to come, it played much better than anyone could have expected.

General Colin L. Powell once said: "General Schwarzkopf is in charge of U.S. forces. We are in the kingdom of Saudi Arabia at the invitation of the government of Saudi Arabia."

Schwarzkopf said: "This is not NATO, okay, there is not one supreme commander, and there doesn't need to be."

Khalid himself said: "My command and General Schwarzkopf's command, actually it's in one headquarters, not two. I believe that it is extremely studied. [We communicate] in English, actually, because first of all, Saudi officers, most of them, they studied in England or, most of them, in the United States.

"For the Arab nations, they take their orders and their communications through our command jointly in Arabic. In most of them, we have liaisons between . . . brigades or battalions or even divisions. And [these] communications we are extremely comfortable with for the time being.''

COMMANDER IN CHIEF, FRENCH COMMAND
LIEUTENANT GENERAL MICHEL ROQUEJEOFFRE

For the French, their inclusion of parts of the famed French Foreign Legion were welcomed by General Schwarzkopf, who knew that they were equal to their reputation and would prove to provide veteran help in the esoteric demands of desert warfare.

By the end of December 1990, most of the troops and matériel were in place. When the Iraqis did not move out of Kuwait by January 15, which was the deadline set by President Bush and the United Nations, the phase of Operation Desert Storm involving the air attack began. That phase continued until February 24, when the so-called ground war phase began.

The visit of Defense Secretary Dick Cheney and Chairman of the Joint Chiefs of Staff Colin L. Powell had sealed the fate of the Iraqi army two weeks previous to that time.

17

General Powell:
Getting Into the Stadium

At the onset of the Coalition Forces' war with Iraq, General Powell, as Chairman of the Joint Chiefs of Staff, was not particularly well disposed toward Saddam Hussein, who earned Powell's scorn for pretending to be a military man even though he had never served a day in any army.

Powell sardonically called him *Mr.* Saddam Hussein, in much the same manner as Winston Churchill in World War II frequently referred scathingly to his opposite number in Berlin as *Corporal* Hitler.

He considered Hussein as about as slimy as you could get. Powell could never care less about how many uniforms Hussein had worn; he knew he had never fought on the ground with real troops. He appeared more as an escapee from a *Saturday Night Live* skit.

In order to get into the mind of Saddam Hussein, as any commander must get into the mind of the enemy, Powell began to hit the history books and studied the classic area that was once called Mesopotamia.

"It takes me back to the period 8000 B.C. in the valleys of the Euphrates and Tigris rivers," he told a reporter about a heavy tome he was carrying. "It's slowly bringing me up to date."

At the time, he said, he had read up to about 4000 B.C. "I'm up to the point of the invention of the Sumerian language. I've got a long way to go.''

He was doing historical research, he said, because "you need touch points. I like to say, 'Guys, let's get into the stadium first before we play ball.' I always like to have a context for what I do, so I know I'm in the right stadium and I'm playing the right game. Then I can go on the field and play it. History helps put me in that context.''

He went on. "Frankly, the only lesson that I can pull out of the history of the Middle East is that it'll never be uncomplicated and that history is not always the best judge of what's liable to happen in the future. These things in the Persian Gulf: for a number of years now we've had a certain balanced set of forces and balanced strategic interests. Now, it's all sort of up.

"I mean, the Syrians are coming to help the Saudis, the Egyptians are there to help the Saudis. The Americans have been allowed into the kingdom. The Soviets are on our side of the issue. The Iranians got everything they didn't win in the war, and they're not giving the Iraqis anything to get at, except that they won't cross the Shatt-al-Arab, at least not right now. You sit down and try to sort all that out.''

He was bowled over by the dramatic changes in the area. "Ten or eleven years ago, if you were talking about the Persian Gulf and the Middle East, one of the great fears we had was that it could lead to superpower confrontation. The United States and the Soviet Union could go to war—with each other—and set the stage for World War III. It's almost ludicrous today to think that anything in the Persian Gulf could lead to the United States and the Soviet Union shooting dice over it, for real. That's a significant change. And that's exciting.''

On August 2, 1990, the day Iraq invaded Kuwait, Powell told President Bush in no uncertain terms: If the U.S. did not retaliate against Iraq with massive force, the U.S. would cease to be a superpower.

That is not to say that Powell was ever a warmonger. Erstwhile Secretary of Defense Frank Carlucci put it this way: "He understands clearly the uses and limitations of military power.

He recognizes the merits of negotiation and would like to get an acceptable negotiated solution. But he will fight if he has to fight.''

Apropos of that, it is interesting to note that America's war with Iraq was the first major war a Republican president involved America in during the twentieth century.

Said one senior Bush official of the Iraqi invasion of Kuwait: "From the very beginning Colin's point has been to go with everything we've got as fast as we can get it there.'' Operation Desert Shield was the largest mobilization of U.S. troops anywhere since the Vietnam War.

Powell always felt as comfortable speaking with the President in the White House as he did with the troops on the field. One of his military associates said, "If there was ever anybody who could communicate with the private fixing a broken tank tread and in the next second talk with the President, it's Colin Powell.''

As if to prove this point, on February 11, 1991, Powell visited the hangar of an F-117A Stealth fighter to the gleeful cheers of the airmen and women present. Stepping up to a two-thousand-pound bomb, pen in hand, Powell inscribed the following message to *Mr*. Saddam Hussein: "You didn't move it, so now you lose it.'' It sounded like a poem by Muhammad Ali on the even of a multimillion-dollar prize fight.

The troops cheered.

Defense Secretary Cheney, also in attendance, wrote on the bomb: "To Saddam with affection.''

The GBU-27, a laser-guided bomb meant to pierce hardened bunkers before blowing up, would be dropped on a target in Iraq.

The troops belonged to the 37th Tactical Fighter Wing, two Stealth fighter squadrons dubbed the "Night Stalkers'' and the "Ghost Riders.''

According to Pentagon officials, there are only fifty-nine Stealth fighters in the world. They attacked 80 percent of the best-defended Iraqi targets.

This particular Stealth was called "Christine'' by its maintenance crew, after a killer car in a minor thriller novel by Stephen King. Explained a technical sergeant, "There's a bug in that plane somewhere that nobody can find. It causes certain things not to work, and certain things to work when they shouldn't work.''

The troops enjoyed the speeches Powell gave them. On February 8, 1991, at an American air base in western Saudi Arabia, Powell addressed the assembled troops after Secretary Cheney had finished.

''I'd just like to add my own words of appreciation to those of the Secretary, and let you know the pride that we feel and the President feels and all Americans feel in what you have been doing here, not only during Operation Desert Storm but before that during Operation Desert Shield. Several weeks ago, we took on the fourth largest armed force in the world, and in a little over three weeks made his air force combat-ineffective, his air defense system combat-ineffective, destroyed what little navy he had by tearing up his lines of communication.

''And now the focus of the battle will shift to the Iraqi army in Kuwait, which is what we came here to do—kick them out. We tried to give him some good advice a few months ago. We told him, 'Move it or lose it.' They wouldn't move it; now they're going to lose it.''

The troops cheered deliriously.

Powell went on with his pep talk. ''And there should be no doubt in anyone's mind, because I know there's no doubt in your mind, that we have the capacity to do that. We brought the armed forces of the United States here—ground power, air power, naval power, marine power. He's seen what our air force can do.

''He's going to see a lot more of it in the days and weeks ahead. We still have very, very capable ground forces that can be put into the battle if necessary and at the right time. And we'll do it to make air power even that much more effective. It'll be a single, integrated campaign.

''We want to get it over with as quickly as possible. We want to do it in a way that minimizes loss of U.S. and allied life, of course. We also want to get it concluded so that you can get back to those who love you at home and who you miss so very much. And I know what it's like to be away from home for a long period of time, and I know the sacrifice that you're making and the sacrifices that your families are making.

"If it's a source of comfort to you, you need to know, really know, that the American people are solidly behind you. You can't believe the level of pride that exists in America for what you're doing, for the kind of performance you're putting in. For years, people wondered whether our equipment would work, whether the all-volunteer force would work, whether we really were trained and ready, whether we really were professionals.

"And in a period of just a few weeks, you've demonstrated that in spades. So that of all the situations in the United States, none stands higher in the eyes of the American people than the armed forces, as a result of what you have been doing over the last several weeks.

"So it's a pleasure to be with you today. We're enormously proud of your contributions. The American people are behind you. We're going to get this thing over with quickly, in a simple process of cut it off and kill it, and then we're going to get home as fast as we can. Thank you very much."

The troops cheered and applauded wildly.

What with Powell's immense popularity, the *Boston Globe*'s Derrick Jackson thought that Powell should run for president in 1996. Jackson wrote that Powell was "perfect for these militaristic times . . . perfect for these telegenic times that Doug Wilder, a more conservative African-American, might get on the Democratic ticket." Powell on the GOP ticket "could make the Democrats gag. Powell can talk immigrant talk. His parents are from Jamaica. He can talk bootstrap. He rose from a C college average to a master's degree in business administration. He can talk macho patriot talk. He has a Purple Heart. He can talk black talk. He always credits his position to the struggle of African-Americans long gone."

In Jackson's opinion, "Many white people, and even some hard-boiled racists, will accept Powell because his authority is invested in carrying out U.S. government policy."

On March 3, 1991, White House Chief of Staff John H. Sununu said there was no chance of Powell replacing Quayle as Vice President on the 1992 GOP ticket. Sununu said on

CNN's *Evans and Novak* show that Powell had "indicated to a number of us that he'd like to be considered for another stint as Chairman of the Joint Chiefs." Sununu also said, "A Bush-Quayle ticket is a lock-solid ticket in 1992. The President has made it clear on other occasions that it is a solid ticket."

Some conservative Republicans had doubts about Powell's being on their ticket because he had endorsed nonmilitary public spending, as in 1989 when he described his life as "the story of the kid of an inner-city immigrant family who benefited from living in a city that treated its obligation to educate and provide for its youth as the most important investment it could make."

After the war was over and General Schwarzkopf's video of his final briefing on the Persian Gulf War had proved to be a blockbuster in the video stores, some wag suggested that he and Powell should do a rap dance video slamming Saddam Hussein.

"Saaa-Daaam, you better watch out! Saaa-Daaam, you better watch out! Who's sane, Hussein? Who's sane, Hussein? Not you! Rap!"

Or, for that matter, what about a Schwarzkopf ticket in 1996?

Pollsters claimed that Powell on Bush's ticket in 1992 would help Bush win New York, where Bush lost in 1988. Powell, who was born in Harlem, would appeal to New Yorkers.

Powell, so far, has been lukewarm to any idea of running for office. His spokesman, Colonel Bill Smullen, pointed out once that Powell had "never stated his political preference" and that he had "no political aspirations. Right now, he has a full-time job keeping him busy."

Nevertheless, political pundits kept speculating about Powell's vote appeal. Analyst Norman Ornstein, for instance, said it was "rising through the roof, through the stars, and out into the stratosphere. Without much exaggeration, we may be talking about another phenomenon more like Eisenhower than any other military figure."

During the first week of combat in the Persian Gulf War, Powell remained calm and patient. He declared that a force of half a million Iraqi soldiers was in the Kuwait theater, "sitting there dug in, waiting to be attacked, and attacked it will be.

We're in no hurry. We are not looking to have large numbers of casualties.''

Meanwhile, Iraqi Scud missiles were flying at Israel and Saudi Arabia and being torn apart in the sky by American Patriot missiles.

Some of the big questions of the war that came up as hostilities persisted were: Why didn't Saddam Hussein use his poisonous gases on American troops? Why didn't he use air fuel bombs? Why didn't his air force challenge Coalition aircraft in the skies over Iraq? Powell had no certain answers to any of these. Much of Hussein's actions—or inactions—remained a puzzle.

Hussein had called this war the ''mother of all battles,'' when in fact it turned out to be the mother of all annihilations. Nobody knew how many Iraqis were killed, but the number was presumed to be well into the thousands, possibly hundreds of thousands, while only approximately one hundred Americans lost their lives. Hussein's troops would rather surrender than fight for Hussein. American air power ''softened'' them up, i.e., killed scores of them, and then they gave up to the Coalition Forces.

As Powell put it, ''This has not been, so far, a very good return on the investment that Saddam Hussein has put into [his] air force.'' To put it mildly.

He went on to say that Coalition air forces ''have free run of the area as much as possible. There still will be losses, and I don't want to understate that. But in general, [we have] air superiority.''

Powell derided the Iraqi navy as a bunch of ''minor and insignificant patrol boats.'' He explained that the air attacks on Baghdad were intended to sever the ''brains of the operation.'' The bombers would ''intensify this cutting-off process'' from Baghdad southward down the Tigris and Euphrates Valley to Basra, the second largest city of Iraq, which harbored the headquarters of the Iraqi forces.

''And,'' said Powell, ''as we get into the process of cutting it off, we will also step up the process of killing it by going after stockpiles, ammunition, food, stripping away their gun air defense, using air attacks, and, if it becomes necessary . . .

assembling a fairly sizable ground force that could finish off the job.''

He added that he was "not telegraphing anything. I just want everybody to know that we have a toolbox that's full of lots of tools. And I brought them all to the party.''

Powell never contended that air power alone would conquer the Iraqi army.

What shocked everybody was the alacrity and outright success of the ground war and the relatively small loss of soldiers on the side of the Coalition Forces. The media had hyped up the war to such an extent that everyone expected Iraq to use poison gas attacks, bacteriological warfare, antitank trenches flooded with flaming oil, kamikaze pilots carrying toxic mustard gas, and other horrific assaults on the allied armies. Instead, Iraq sent Scuds, which for the most part missed their targets, but caused a lot of damage in landing in untargeted areas.

Unlike Vietnam, the Persian Gulf War did not allow the media to roam freely about the landscape and view the battle-grounds in action. The media complained bitterly about not getting enough information from the government, which defended itself by claiming national security was at stake and therefore information to the public had to be carefully censored.

Walter Cronkite, the old war-horse who had covered Vietnam and other wars, wrote a plaintive piece for *Newsweek* titled "What Is There to Hide?" The editorial was subtitled: "Military Arrogance Keeps the Public in the Dark."

"With an arrogance foreign to the democratic system, the U.S. military in Saudi Arabia is trampling on the American people's right to know," he began—the sampling enough to indicate the tone and direction of the argument.

Powell, however, got rave reviews for his briefing on the Gulf War. The media could not get enough of him.

He was even looking ahead to a time after the war was done to project future security arrangements that might be necessary in the Persian Gulf region. He said on January 10, 1991, "It's a little hard to tell right now, but it seems to me it'll have to be something different than the arrangement that has existed previously. You should not draw from that statement that there's going to be a large U.S. presence indefinitely.

"I think there are ways to provide security to the region after the event, should the event be necessary, but we will probably have more of a presence in the region, perhaps at sea, perhaps with marine forces, perhaps with pre-positioning, perhaps with exercises, perhaps with command control installations, but it's early—still premature, rather early—to talk about what that arrangement would look like, what role the UN would play and what role our friends in the region would want us to play.

"And so we're giving this considerable thought, but it's—it's still rather early to get very definitive about it."

At the beginning of the war Powell thought the Iraqis had an imposing fighting force of one million hard-bitten soldiers, tempered by their hitch in the Iran-Iraq war. Powell told the District of Columbia Bar Association in Washington in 1991:

"I don't believe that we are either underestimating or overestimating the armed forces of Iraq. One million soldiers, six thousand tanks. They have shown a degree of sophistication that is impressive. They fought war against Iran for eight years and prevailed. . . . Some parts of the force are very competent, very well led, paid more, get the best equipment. Other parts of the force are much, much less capable, and the so-called new forces that have been mobilized in recent weeks are even less capable.

"And so we view them as a potential worthy opponent, and without getting into any details, the strategy that we are looking at will deal with the stress we know they have and will also exploit the weaknesses we know that they have, and I think that's as far as I wish to go right now."

In the Q & A session that followed, the following exchange occurred:

Q. It's been speculated that Saddam Hussein is a student of the U.S. experience in Vietnam. Some members of our audience have asked me, What do you think the lessons of the Vietnam experience are for the United States? and How [have they] been applied in connection with Desert Shield?

A. It's a frequent question, and I frankly don't sit around late at night worrying about Vietnam or the lessons of Vietnam. Lessons come out of every conflict, every war, every crisis, and you can't go back to one and try to model the future against that particular crisis. You essentially develop a body of thinking and theory about it all.

And what we are doing in Desert Shield is unique to Desert Shield, and is not just dragging up the lessons learned from Vietnam or Panama or anywhere else. We've studied the theater we're in, we've studied the potential enemy, we have looked at our capabilities. We have gone with our whole toolbox and not just a part of our toolbox, and so I'm approaching this, and the members of the Joint Chiefs of Staff and our commanders are approaching this, as a stand-alone military operation.

And, frankly, the lessons that I have discovered most appropriate to Desert Shield are lessons that I've learned throughout my career and not as a result of any particular Vietnam experience.

But so that I'm not entirely dodging your question, one of the things that we do reflect on a little bit is, Are we being supported by the American people in this effort? And although there is uncertainty and concern out there—as there should be where there is a possibility of war—I'm pleased with the level of support that our GIs are receiving from the American people, and that means a great deal to those of us in uniform who may be sent in harm's way.

Here Powell showed that he was intelligent enough to know that going around comparing every crisis or war to Vietnam would get no one anywhere. Why did history have to revolve around Vietnam? In fact, it didn't. Vietnam was an anomaly— a grain of sand on the beach of history.

During the Persian Gulf War, Powell acted as an intermediary between President Bush and General Schwarzkopf. For example, Schwarzkopf asked Powell at every turn to warn administration officials against rushing the military into combat before it was ready. As can be seen, Powell acted as the

Washington-based political head of the military in the Persian Gulf War, whereas Schwarzkopf acted as the actual head of the military forces in the Gulf.

Powell did, of course, visit the troops in Saudia Arabia. He did not stay closeted in the Pentagon and White House all the time. For example, he visited grunts in Riyadh, Saudi Arabia, on Christmas Day, 1990.

When Powell offered his hand to Army Specialist Garth Flowers, Flowers plunked a sandbag in it. He had not recognized Powell. He thought he was just another GI in the sandbag brigade. Flowers's heart stopped when he recognized the Chairman of the Joint Chiefs of Staff. He figured his career was down the tubes. Powell coolly took no umbrage. In fact, he smiled and slammed the sandbag into a bunker as he wished Flowers a Merry Christmas.

In other words, Powell could fit in so well with his troops that they sometimes didn't even recognize him. This attribute made him extremely popular with the troops.

It is important to stress that Powell as Chairman of the Joint Chiefs did *not* make foreign policy. President Bush was and is the Commander in Chief of the U.S. armed forces and *he* made policy. Powell simply carried out Bush's orders.

For example, it was President Bush who made the ultimate decision to oust Noriega from power in Panama. It was Powell who carried out Bush's will by corralling Noriega when he sought sanctuary in the papal nuncio in Panama—a kind of ludicrous reprise of Quasimodo's quest for safety in Victor Hugo's *The Hunchback of Notre Dame*. (At the time of this writing, Noriega is sitting in a Miami prison awaiting his trial on drug-trafficking charges.)

The President never made any bones about his desire to see Saddam Hussein totally out of power. One always got the impression that Bush enjoyed his role of generalissimo. If you were on his Ten Most Wanted List, your days as a leader were probably numbered. Bush's thinking led him to believe that if he got rid of the enemy leader of a country, he would solve the problem of that leader's actions.

Actually, Bush liked to reduce everything to an ad hominem

conflict. He knew it played well for the media and the public. It allowed the public to focus its hatred on a person rather than on an entire country or an ideology—both of which usually proved too abstract to hate. It was easier to fume with hatred for a person than for an idea. Bertrand Russell put it in a nutshell: people aren't happy unless they have somebody to hate.

Concentrating hatred on Hussein also diverted public perception away from one of the several reasons for the war: oil. After all, everyone knew that Bush's forebears were Texas wildcatters. Oil ran in his family. All modern industrialized nations needed oil to function. Bush knew he could not allow Hussein to corner the oil market—and the Iraqi leader was definitely on his way to doing it when he rammed through the Iraq-Kuwait border and seized Kuwait City.

For then Hussein could hold the industrialized world hostage to his will. Did Hussein really think he had a prayer going up against the entire industrialized world? Especially without any air power?

Powell, for one, was proud of America's air attacks on Iraq. At the end of the first week, Coalition Forces had flown more than 10,000 air sorties in carrying out the biggest air campaign in history.

Said Powell in February 1991: "I think we have been awfully good in avoiding collateral damage," the latter phrase a euphemism for civilian casualties. He was right, relatively speaking. Compared to the Allied bombing of Dresden in World War II, which resulted in the wholesale slaughter of civilians, the Persian Gulf War did avoid excessive "collateral damage."

Powell never downplayed the effectiveness of Iraq's army in front of the media. At one briefing he said, "We're dealing with an enemy that is resourceful . . . that is ingenious." High praise indeed for an army that inflicted hardly any casualties on the Coalition Forces.

According to Elizabeth Drew in *The New Yorker* magazine, Powell wanted an early and strong buildup of forces in the Middle East so as to avoid a Vietnam-type situation in which the generals would be forced to keep asking for more and more troops in an obvious escalation of a war that was going badly.

Powell was implementing his hit-them-with-everything-you've-got philosophy.

Powell never said that the war would be easy. If anything, he overestimated the amount of time and force that would be necessary to finish the job.

One of his most characteristic actions was to emphasize continually the role of General H. Norman Schwarzkopf in the planning of Operation Desert Storm. Defense Secretary Cheney, agreeing with Powell, said once that the operation was "basically Norm's plan. It's fundamentally Norm's to execute."

Powell gave credit where credit was due. He never tried to steal the limelight from Schwarzkopf. Stealing the limelight from Schwarzkopf, in view of the way Schwarzkopf came off with the public, would have been another Vietnam no-win war in itself!

On his visit to Riyadh, Saudi Arabia, with Cheney on December 25, 1990, Powell did catch flak from some of the soldiers, a rather unusual turn of events. When Powell told the pilots of tank-killing A-10 jets, "It's going to be fun if it ever gets started," Staff Sergeant Armando Graham could hardly believe his ears.

"What's going to be fun?" Graham wondered out loud. *"He's* not going to be here."

No hard feelings, though. Graham was among the first batch of GIs to ask Powell for an autograph when they mobbed him with magazines, Saudi currency, a skateboard, and almost anything they could get their hands on.

Powell cheerfully obliged.

On another day in Riyadh, Powell stopped and chatted with the army's 59th Chemical Company, 101st Corps Support Group, and the four enlisted women who were there giggled and shrieked as they posed for snapshots with Powell.

"I touched his arm! I touched his arm!" one screamed, as if she were touching rock star David Bowie.

Front-line troops asked Powell questions like, "Sir, is it possible for us to get the M-60-E2 machine gun?" and "Where and how would a light-infantry unit be used against the main armored threat?"

He told them they would get everything they needed and when it came to a fight with Saddam Hussein they would "challenge him in ways he's never seen before."

Powell commiserated with the troops when he said he knew of "the thoughts you're given late at night and how your stomach turns over it."

He added, "Stay with us, keep being the professionals you've been so far, and we'll take care of your families until you get home safely."

When he toured the army's Central Command port facilities, he called them a "logistician's dream and a logistician's nightmare."

On his travels, Powell saw rafts of Apache and Chinook helicopters and hundreds of M1A1 tanks from Germany, the most powerful tanks in the American arsenal. The tanks, freshly off-loaded, were still painted forest green. In no time they would set out for the "tanning salon," the soldiers' term for a coat of sand-colored paint that would make it almost impossible for the tanks to be distinguished from the miles and miles of real sand against which they might be sighted by Iraqi gunners.

At home on his haunches under camouflage netting with Charlie Company, just one of the guys, General Colin L. Powell tore open the foil around a Meal-Ready-to-Eat and shared chicken a la king with the troops.

Less than two months later, in early February 1991, Powell was in the Saudi desert again with Defense Secretary Cheney, talking to the troops, but rather more importantly, talking to H. Norman Schwarzkopf about a time schedule for the ground-war phase of Operation Desert Storm.

It was at that meeting that Powell and Schwarzkopf established a window for a D-Day H-Hour initiation of the ground war—extending from about February 21 to February 24. The final selection of the exact date would be up to Commander in Chief Bush in concert with Field Commander Schwarzkopf.

What occurred on the battlefield after the commencement of the ground-war phase of battle could not be described in detail by anyone better than the man who had imagined it, nurtured it, developed it, and brought it to final fruition:

General H. Norman Schwarzkopf.

On February 27, 1991, he told the world how his troops had brought the Iraqis to their knees.

18

General Schwarzkopf: Desert Storm Strategy

The following are remarks made by General H. Norman Schwarzkopf during a press briefing February 27, 1991, in Riyadh, Saudi Arabia.

"I promised some of you all a few days ago that as soon as the opportunity presented itself, I would give you a complete rundown on what we were doing, and, more importantly, why we were doing it; the strategy behind what we were doing. I've been asked by [Defense] Secretary [Richard B.] Cheney to do that this evening, and so, if you will bear with me, we're going to go through a briefing. . . .

"As you recall, we started our deployment on [August 7]. Basically, what we started out against was a couple of hundred thousand Iraqis that were in the Kuwait theater of operation. I don't have to remind you all that we brought over initially defensive forces, in the form of the 101st [Airborne Division], the 82nd [Airborne Division], the 24th Mechanized Infantry Division, the 3rd Armored Cavalry, and, in essence, we had them arrayed to the south behind the Saudi task force. Also, there were Arab forces over here in this area arrayed in defensive positions."

Schwarzkopf pointed to a line of troops just south of Kuwait on the briefing map.

"And that, in essence, is the way we started. In the middle

of November, the decision was made to increase the force because by that time huge numbers of Iraq forces had flowed into the area and generally in the disposition as they're shown here, and therefore, we increased the forces and built up more forces.''

"I would tell you that at this time we made a very deliberate decision to align all of those forces within the boundary looking north toward Kuwait. . . . We also at that time had a very active naval presence out in the gulf. And we made sure that everybody understood about that naval presence. One of the reasons why we did that is because it became very apparent to us early on that the Iraqis were quite concerned about an amphibious operation across the shores to liberate Kuwait. . . . They put a very, very heavy barrier of infantry along here and then proceeded to build an extensive barrier that went all the way across the border, down, and around, and up the side of Kuwait.

"Basically, the problem we were faced with was this: when you looked at the troop numbers, they really outnumbered us about three to two. And when you consider the number of combat service support people we had, that's logisticians and that sort of thing, in our armed forces, as far as fighting troops, we were really outnumbered two to one. In addition to that, they had 4,700 tanks versus our 3,500 when the buildup was complete, and they had a great deal more artillery than we do.

"I think any student of military strategy would tell you that in order to attack a position, you should have a ratio of approximately three to one in favor of the attacker. And, in order to attack a position that is heavily dug in and barricaded, such as the one we had here, you should have a ratio of five to one in the way of troops in favor of the attacker. So you can see basically what our problem was at that time. We were outnumbered, at a minimum, three to two as far as troops were concerned; we were outnumbered as far as tanks were concerned; and we had to come up with some way to make up the difference. . . .

"What we did, of course, was start an extensive air campaign, and I briefed you in quite some detail on that in the past. One of the purposes I told you at that time of that extensive air campaign was to isolate the Kuwaiti theater of operation by taking out all the bridges and supply lines that ran between the north and the southern part of Iraq. That was to prevent reinforcement and supply coming into the southern part of Iraq and the Kuwaiti theater of operation.

"We also conducted a very heavy bombing campaign, and many people questioned why—why the extensive bombing campaign. This is the reason why. It was necessary to reduce these forces down to a strength that made them weaker, particularly along the front-line barrier that we had to go through.

"We continued our heavy operations out in the sea because we wanted the Iraqis to continue to believe that we were going to conduct a massive amphibious operation. . . . And I think many of you recall the number of amphibious rehearsals we had, to include Imminent Thunder that was written about quite extensively for many reasons. But we continued to have those operations because we wanted him [Saddam Hussein] to concentrate his forces, which he did.

"I think this is probably one of the most important parts of the entire briefing I could talk about. As you know, very early on, we took out the Iraqi air force. We knew that he [Hussein] had very, very limited reconnaissance means. And therefore, when we took out his air force, for all intents and purposes we took out his ability to see what we were doing down here in Saudi Arabia.

"Once we had taken out his eyes, we did what could best be described as the Hail Mary play in football. I think you recall, when the quarterback is desperate for a touchdown at the very end [of a close game], what he does is, he steps up behind the center, and all of a sudden every single one of his receivers goes way out to one flank, and they all run down the field as fast as they possibly can and into the end zone, and he lobs the ball. In essence that's what we did."

"When we knew he couldn't see us anymore, we did a massive movement of troops all the way out to the west, to the extreme west, because at that time we knew he was still fixed in this area with the vast majority of his forces, and once the air campaign started, he would be incapable of moving out to counter this move, even if he knew we made it.

"There were some additional troops out in this area [Iraqi

territory west of Kuwait], but they did not have the capability or the time to put in the barrier that had been described by Saddam Hussein as an absolutely impenetrable tank barrier that no one would ever get through; I believe those were his words.

"So this was absolutely an extraordinary move, I must tell you. I can't recall any time in the annals of military history when this number of forces have moved over this distance to put themselves in a position to be able to attack. . . . But what's more important—and I think it's very, very important that I make this point—and that's these logistics bases. Not only did we move the troops out there, but we literally moved thousands and thousands of tons of fuel, of ammunition, of spare parts, of water and food, out here into this area, because we wanted to have enough supplies on hand so that if we launched this and if we got into a slugfest battle, which we very easily could have gotten into, we'd have enough supplies to last for sixty days.

"So it was an absolutely gigantic accomplishment, and I can't give credit enough to the logisticians and the transporters who were able to pull this off, to the superb support we had from the Saudi government, the literally thousands and thousands of drivers, really, of every national origin, who helped us in this move out here. And, of course, great credit goes to the commanders of these units who were also able to maneuver their forces out here and put them in this position.

"But as a result, by [February 23], what you found is this situation. The front lines had been attrited down to a point where all of these units were at 50 percent or below. The second level, basically, that we had to face—and these were the real tough fighters that we were worried about right here—were attrited to someplace between 50 and 75 percent, although we still had the Republican Guard located here and here, and part of the Republican Guard in this area, they were very strong, and the Republican Guard up in this area, strong.

"And we continued to hit the bridges all across this area to make absolutely sure that no more reinforcements came into the battle. This was the situation on [February 23]. Oh, wait . . . I shouldn't forget these fellows. . . . We put Special Forces deep into the enemy territory. They went out on strategic reconnaissance for us. And they let us know what was going on out there, and they were the eyes that were out there, and it's very important that I not forget those folks.''

"This, then, was the morning of [February 24]. Our plan initially had been to start over here in this area (the Kuwait-Iraq border) and do exactly what the Iraqis thought we were going to do, and that's take them on head-on into their most heavily defended area. Also, at the same time, we launched amphibious flanks and naval gunfire in this area (southern Kuwait) so that they continued to think that we were going to be attacking along this coast, and therefore fixed their forces in this position. Our hope was that by fixing the forces in this position and with this attack through here, we would basically keep the forces here and they wouldn't know what was going on out in this area.'' Schwarzkopf was pointing to an area west of Kuwait in Iraq.

"And I believe we succeeded in that very well. At four o'clock in the morning, the marines, the 1st Marine Division and the 2nd Marine Division, launched attacks through the barrier system. They were accompanied by the Tiger Brigade, U.S. Army Tiger Brigade of the 2nd Armored Division. At the same time, two Saudi task forces also launched a penetration through this barrier.

"But while they were doing that, at four o'clock in the morning over here, the 6th French Armored Division, accompanied by a brigade of the 82nd Airborne, also launched an overland attack to their objective up in this area, Al Salman airfield. And we were held up a little bit by the weather, but by eight o'clock in the morning, the 101st Airborne Air Assault launched an air assault deep in the enemy territory to establish a forward operating base in this location right here.''

Schwarzkopf indicated an area in eastern Iraq.

"Let me talk about each one of those moves.

"First of all, the Saudis over here on the east coast did a terrific job. They went up against a very, very tough barrier system. They breached the barrier very, very effectively. They moved out aggressively and continued their attack up the coast.

"I can't say enough about the two marine divisions. If I use words like *brilliant*, it would really be an under-description of the absolutely superb job that they did in breaching the so-called impenetrable barrier. It was a classic, absolutely classic military breaching of a very, very touch mine field, barbed wire, fire trenches-type barrier. They went through the first barrier like it was water. They went across into the second barrier line, even though they were under artillery fire at the time. They continued to open up that breach. And then they brought both divisions streaming through that breach. Absolutely superb operation, as textbook, and I think it'll be studied for many, many years to come as the way to do it.

"I would also like to say that the French did an absolutely superb job of moving out rapidly to take their objective out here (eastern Iraq) and they were very, very successful, as was the 101st.

"What we found was as soon as we breached these obstacles here and started bringing pressure, we started getting a large number of surrenders. . . . We were worried about the weather. The weather, it turned out, was going to get pretty bad the next day, and we were worried about launching this air assault. And we also started to have a huge number of atrocities, of really the most unspeakable type, committed in downtown Kuwait City, to include reports that the desalination plant had been destroyed. And when we heard that, we were quite concerned about what might be going on.

"Based upon that and the situation as it was developing, we made a decision that rather than wait until the following morning to launch the remainder of these forces, that we would go ahead and launch those forces that afternoon."

Schwarzkopf switched to a new map.

"This was the situation you saw the afternoon of [February 24]. The marines continued to make great progress going through the breach in this area and were moving rapidly north. The Saudi task force on the east coast was also moving rapidly to the north and making very, very good progress.

"We launched another Egyptian-Arab force in this location and another Saudi force in this location, again to penetrate the barrier, but once again to make the enemy continue to think that we're doing exactly what he wanted us to do, and that's make a headlong assault into a very, very tough barrier system, a very, very tough mission for these folks here.

"But at the same time, what we did was continue to attack with the French. We continued—we launched an attack on the part of the entire VII Corps where the 1st Infantry Division went through, breached an obstacle and mine-field barrier here, established quite a large breach, through which we passed the 1st British Armored Division. At the same time, we launched the 1st Armored Division, the 3rd Armored Division, and because of our deception plan and the way it worked, we didn't even have to worry about a barrier. We just went right around the enemy and were behind him in no time at all.

"The 2nd Armored Cavalry Division and the 24th Mech Division also launched out here in the far west. And I ought to talk about the 101st because this is an important point.

"Once the 101st had their forward operating base established here, they then went ahead and launched into the Tigris and the Euphrates Valley. There's a lot of people who are still saying that the object of the United States of America was to capture Iraq and cause the downfall of the entire country of Iraq.

"Ladies and gentlemen, when we were here (Kuwait), we were 150 miles away from Baghdad, and there was nobody between us and Baghdad. If it had been our intention to take Iraq, if it had been our intention to destroy the country, if it had been our intention to overrun the country, we could have done it unopposed for all intents and purposes from this position at that time. But that was not our intention. We had never said it was our intention. Our intention was purely to eject the Iraqis out of Kuwait and to destroy the military power that had come in here."

Schwarzkopf called for the next map.

"The next two days went exactly like we thought they could go. The Saudis continued to make great progress up on the eastern flank, keeping the pressure off the marines on the flank here; the special forces went out and started operating small-boat operations out in this area to help clear mines but also to threaten the flanks here and to continue to make them think that we were, in fact, going to conduct amphibious operations.

"The Saudi . . . and Arab forces that came in and took these two initial objectives turned out to come in on the flank heading toward Kuwait City. . . . The British . . . passed through and continued to attack up this flank, and, of course, the VII Corps came in and attacked in this direction, as shown here. The 24th Infantry Division made an unbelievable move all the way across into the Tigris and Euphrates Valley and proceeded in blocking this avenue of egress . . . which was the only avenue of egress left because we continued to make sure that the bridges stayed down. So, there was no way out once the 24th was in this area and the 101st continued to operate in here.

"The French, having succeeded in achieving all of their objectives, then set up a flanking position, a flank guard position here to make sure that no forces came in and got us from the flank. By this time, we had destroyed or rendered completely ineffective over twenty-one Iraqi divisions.

"And, of course, that then brings us to today. Where we are today is we now have a solid wall across the north of the XVIII Airborne Corps, consisting of the units shown right here, attacking straight to the east; we have a solid wall here, again, of the VII Corps, also attacking straight to the east. The forces that they are fighting right now are the forces of the Republican Guard.

"Again, today, we had a very significant day when the Arabs coming from the west and the east closed in and moved in to Kuwait City, where they are now in the process of clearing Kuwait City entirely and assuring that it's absolutely secure. The 1st Marine Division continues to hold Kuwaiti International Airport; the 2nd Marine Division continues to be in a position where it blocks any egress out of the city of Kuwait, so no one can leave. To date, we have destroyed over twenty-nine—destroyed or rendered [them] inoperable; I don't like to say 'destroyed' because that gives you the visions of absolutely killing everyone, and that's not what we are doing—but we have rendered completely ineffective over twenty-nine Iraqi divisions, and the gates are closed. There was no way out of here; there was no way out of here; and the enemy is fighting us in this location right here.

"We continue, of course, to have overwhelming air power.

The air has done a terrific job from start to finish in supporting the ground forces, and we also have had great support from the navy, both in the form of naval gunfire and in the support of carrier air. That's the situation at the present time. . . .

"Peace is not without a cost. These have been the U.S. casualties to date. Now, I would just like to comment briefly about that. . . . The loss of one human life is intolerable to any of us who are in the military. But I would tell you that casualties of that order of magnitude, considering the job that's been done and the number of forces that are involved, are almost miraculous as far as the light number of casualties. It will never be miraculous for the families of those people, but it is miraculous. . . .

"This is what's happened to date with the Iraqis. They started out with over 4,000 tanks; as of today, we have over 3,000 confirmed destroyed, and I do mean destroyed or captured. And, as a matter of fact, that number is low because you can add 700 to that as a result of a battle that's going on right now with the Republican Guard. So, that number is very, very high, and we've almost completely destroyed the offensive capability of the Iraqi forces in the Kuwaiti theater of operation. The armored-vehicle count is also very, very high. And, of course, you can see we're doing great damage to the artillery. The battle is still going on, and I suspect that these numbers will mount rather considerably. . . .

"We're very, very confident that we have well over 50,000 prisoners of war at this time, and that number is mounting on a continuing basis.

"I would remind you that the war is continuing to go on, even as we speak right now. There's fighting going on out there. Even as we speak right now, there are incredible acts of bravery going on. This afternoon we have an F-16 pilot shot down. We had contact with him. He had a broken leg on the ground.

"Two helicopters from the 101st, they didn't have to do it, but they went in to try and pull that pilot out. One of them was shot down, and we're still in the process of working through that. But that's the kind of thing that's going on out on that battlefield right now.

"It is not a Nintendo game. It is a tough battlefield where people are risking their lives at all times, and great heroes are out there, and we ought to all be very, very proud of them.

"That's the campaign to date. That's the strategy to date."

19

Powell and Schwarzkopf: A Tabletop Battle

The Persian Gulf War ended as it began—with full confidence on the part of the Coalition Forces going into battle, and with a specific goal to be reached by engaging in that battle. And when the goal was reached, when, that is, the Iraqi forces were driven out of Kuwait, the war was over.

It was a war that no one questioned would go down in the books as a textbook case, "a tabletop battle," as one American officer, Colonel Paul Murtha of the 18th Aviation Brigade, labeled it. "It's a classic tank-air battle from the textbooks, a tabletop battle."

It was a war that historians and moralists would be arguing about for years. Was it just? Was it imperialist? Was it the birth of a new world? Was it the death knell for all Third World dictators?

Nine men sat in the Oval Office of the White House after lunch on Wednesday, February 27, trying to sort out in their own minds what they had achieved—they and the half-million Coalition Forces in Saudi Arabia, Iraq, and what was left of Kuwait.

General Colin L. Powell, Chairman of the Joint Chiefs of Staff, was there as one of the primary architects of the textbook victory—for which he had worked directly throughout with his alter ego in the field, General H. Norman "The Bear"

Schwarzkopf. As Powell had predicted, the Coalition Forces had used deception and superior speed to trap the Iraqis, and had then killed them.

President Bush had called this meeting of his war cabinet feeling quite confident that things had gone exceedingly well since he had given the signal to start the ground war—Operation Saber—but when he had scheduled it earlier, he had no concept of how close to victory he already was at that moment.

It was Powell who got out the folders of maps and graphs and delivered the stunning, mind-boggling update. After fewer than four full days of ground battle, he said, Iraq was a routed force. *Routed!* The troops of Saddam Hussein were on the run all over Kuwait and all over southern Iraq. The vaunted Republican Guard of the Iraqis was "destroyed"; Operation Desert Storm was virtually a triumph for the Coalition Forces.

Then Bush announced that if the facts were as they seemed to be, that indeed if the Iraqi army was moving out of Kuwait, he wanted to bring the conflict to an end immediately. Someone suggested that the terms for a cease-fire could be worked out overnight in consultation with CentCom and General Schwarzkopf, plus, of course, the leaders of the Coalition Forces in Saudi Arabia. Then the announcement of the successful conclusion of the war could be made first thing on Thursday morning.

"I'd like to do it tonight," Bush said stubbornly.

No one disagreed. One war cabinet member beamed, pointing out that a midnight cease-fire would mean that the ground war had lasted exactly one hundred hours.

However, there was a question. Would CentCom agree? Would the field general in charge of the war agree? Every eye focused on Powell. He smiled, got up, reached in the bottom drawer of the President's desk for the direct line to Riyadh headquarters, and within seconds was chatting with The Bear.

Although neither man knew it, the winds of controversy that had always seemed to hover over the formidable figure of H. Norman Schwarzkopf like the black cloud of despair over Charlie Brown were beginning to puff out their cheeks to subject him to a hurricane's fury.

The quiet discussion between Powell and Schwarzkopf covered a number of important details in relation to the timing of a possible cease-fire. First the two generals talked about the military objectives they had had in mind from the beginning. Whether or not those objectives had been met was never in question. Indeed, they both agreed, as Schwarzkopf said later, that "the appropriate time was coming in the very near future to stop the battle."

There seemed no disagreement between the generals, and after a bit more discussion with the President, Powell was once again on the phone to Schwarzkopf with the President's specific request for a midnight cease-fire.

"What do you think about this time?" Powell asked Schwarzkopf.

"Hey, that's great," Schwarzkopf replied. "I agree."

And thus the decision was made.

In the distance the winds were beginning to stir. Within weeks they would be howling. The controversy centered on the decision for the midnight cease-fire. In a widely telecast postwar interview with David Frost, Schwarzkopf was asked: "How were you consulted about the cease-fire?"

After explaining the details of the main objectives that had been achieved, Schwarzkopf said, "After the third day . . . we knew we had them." Then he thought about that. "You know, we didn't *declare* a cease-fire. What we did is, we suspended offensive operations. Frankly, my recommendation had been, you know, continue the march. I mean, we had them in a rout and we could have continued to . . . reap great destruction upon them. We could have completely closed the door and made it in fact a battle of annihilation.

"And the President, you know, made the decision that . . . we should stop at a given time, at a given place that did leave some escape routes open for them to get back out. . . . I think it was a very humane decision and a very courageous decision on his part also."

The key phrase "my recommendation had been . . . continue the march" stirred the leaves in the trees and soon began bending the branches and the trunks. Almost immediately White House officials called the Pentagon and Powell was on the phone to Schwarzkopf, but The Bear was apparently en route to Bahrain on business.

Cheney issued a statement saying that Schwarzkopf had made no recommendation to continue the war, and in fact concurred with Powell that "we had achieved our military objectives" and there was no need to continue the fighting.

As President Bush climbed into his helicopter on his way to Camp David, some journalist shouted out: "Where's General Schwarzkopf? In the guardhouse?"

Bush waved it off with a smile. "He's got my full support," he called out.

Meanwhile Schwarzkopf had returned to his headquarters and was agonizing over finding his foot once again in his mouth. Powell had been right. It was Powell who had relayed earlier warnings from the Pentagon to Schwarzkopf to keep his public profile low, low, low—particularly now that everything was all over. But it was, in effect, such a visible profile that it was difficult to get it down low enough to keep it out of sight.

Later, President Bush telephoned the general to tell him that he had great confidence in him.

"I am extremely sorry for the poor choice of words on my part that in any way would result in dishonor cast upon you," Schwarzkopf said.

Bush said that he knew Schwarzkopf had in no way intended to criticize him.

"I'm telling you, just forget it," Bush said. "It's not important."

Schwarzkopf told the press: "Since he's my boss, and he told me to forget it, I'm going to forget it."

But it was difficult to do. As an afterthought, Schwarzkopf came out with a personal statement.

"If I could do the whole thing all over again, I know I would change the word 'recommend' to say 'we initially planned.' Because that's what it was. We initially planned to do one thing." The fact that the unexpected success of the ground operation changed things meant that the "initial plan" could be tossed out the window.

To lay the whole thing to rest, Schwarzkopf said:

"Generals aren't in the business of commenting on the correctness or incorrectness of the President's decisions. Anybody who thinks he should be able to do that ought to be fired on the spot."

But on that night of February 27, the media flap was in the future. There was agreement that, from a military perspective, a cease-fire could occur at any time.

President Bush immediately drafted a statement and faxed it to world leaders in the various capitals of the Coalition countries. By the time the meeting had broken up, Downing Street had already received a fax of Bush's planned statement and Bush was on the telephone with John Major, Prime Minister of Britain, scribbling down various changes in the wording.

Bush was soon in touch directly with Francois Mitterrand, the French president, and Brian Mulroney, the Canadian prime minister. He told them what the situation was and asked their opinions. Secretary of State James Baker contacted the Soviet foreign minister, Alexander Bessmertnykh, and Javier Perez de Cuellar, the UN secretary-general.

At nine that night, Bush addressed the world:

"Kuwait is liberated. Iraq's army is defeated. I am pleased to announce that at midnight tonight, exactly one hundred hours since ground operations commenced and six weeks since the start of Operation Desert Storm, all United States and Coalition Forces will suspend offensive combat operations."

The news had spread instantly, hours before, in Saudi Arabia after Schwarzkopf received the word from Powell of President Bush's message-to-be-delivered. His staff members were jubilant.

But no one was more jubilant than The Bear himself. He and his men had been studying desert campaigns carefully for months in an effort to work out the best approach to take. Schwarzkopf admitted many times that he was haunted by the image of General George Patton when he overextended himself trying to relieve the paratroops at Arnheim in the Battle of the Bulge during World War II.

"General Schwarzkopf told me, 'Don't get left in the dust,' " said Major General William Pagonis, the logistics commander of Operation Desert Storm. "By that he meant don't get caught by a fast advance that would outrun the supplies."

It was the swiftness of the victory that startled and frightened Schwarzkopf, even though he had always known he would win the battle. Why? Or, as David Frost asked him: "Did you feel that God was on your side in this war?"

Schwarzkopf nodded. "He had to be. . . . I'll never forget, as long as I live, Gary Luck, the commander of the 18th Airborne Corps, which was the further west corps, that absolutely charged out across, and we were in the Euphrates Valley. . . . Gary called me on the phone, and we were talking . . . 'Well, I want to report to you.' And I said, 'What's your report?' And he said, 'Well, we've captured 3,200 prisoners so far, and they're just streaming in, and we've accomplished all of our objectives, and we're in the Euphrates Valley with the 101st.' And I said, 'Okay, fine.' And I was waiting for the other shoe to fall. And he said, 'Now, let me tell you about our casualties.' And I said, 'Okay.' He said, 'We have one wounded in action.' ' "

Schwarzkopf leaned back and just beamed. "I mean, now," he told Frost, "can you imagine? One wounded in action at that time?"

And that, of course, was "God on our side" to Schwarzkopf.

Schwarzkopf's interest in magic—he was at one time a full-fledged member of the International Brotherhood of Magicians—had inspired him to direct the eye of the Iraqi army to certain details that would lead it to anticipate an amphibious assault off the eastern Kuwaiti coast, plus a frontal attack against the Kuwaiti-Saudi border south of Kuwait City. At the same time, of course, the *real* attack would occur elsewhere.

To do this, Schwarzkopf had employed a magician's strategy: he had massed large numbers of troops in plain sight exactly at the spot where such an assault would be launched. These troops and matériel were always in the sight of the hundreds of Iraqis hunkered down behind the berms along the Kuwaiti-Saudi border.

At the heart of the deception was a British unit called Rhino Force. Rhino Force was the noisiest, most conspicuous unit of troops in the Persian Gulf battlefield. All day and all night the Iraqis would hear the rumble and clank of tanks, radios crackling and orders for deployment and movement being called out, the crump of artillery fire, and so on. Clouds of dust and smoke obscured the action in the daytime—but the huge army force was absolutely *there*.

Rhino Force was a phony. Or would *become* a phony.

What Schwarzkopf's British troops did was tape the sounds of radio traffic from the series of field exercises conducted by the 1st Armored Division in the weeks before the ground war began. All these tapes were played constantly and were being picked up by Iraqi signal intelligence units.

Meanwhile, after the signal went up to begin Operation Saber, the ground war, British forces quietly moved west to join the U.S. 78th Army Corps waiting to attack on the Iraqi-Saudi border. The *tapes* from the earlier deployments when the tanks were moving *east* into position were replayed, and, of course, the Iraqis monitoring the radios thought that *more* tanks were coming to join the first.

One more point should be made about Schwarzkopf's strategy. He had placed his army in a position to indicate that it would attack north from Saudi Arabia directly against the Kuwaiti border. This would indicate that he was going to use heavy force against defended force. But what would happen if Saddam Hussein and his Republican Guard moved one step ahead of Schwarzkopf and *guessed* that this was a trick?

"What was Saddam Hussein's biggest mistake?" Barbara Walters asked Schwarzkopf.

"His predictability," Schwarzkopf answered without hesitation.

"His predictability?" Walters was surprised. "I always thought he was so unpredictable. Everybody says we don't know him. We don't know what makes him do things."

Schwarzkopf shook his head. "We studied the Iran-Iraq campaigns very, very carefully, and, based upon Iran-Iraq campaigns, we came up with a lot of assumptions about what [the Iraqis] would do, an we weren't wrong a single time."

No. Schwarzkopf and Powell were right, because the Iran-Iraq war had demonstrated conclusively that the Iraqis favored a dug-in, mass-against-mass, hunkered-down type of war, a kind of World War I trench war revisited. And because they *favored* it, they psychologically *hoped* they would be fighting that kind of war against the Coalition Forces.

And so, with the Iraqi army programmed to accept the Coalition attack on the strongly fortified border of Kuwait—and against the mined fields and beaches by way of the seafront to the east of Kuwait City—Schwarzkopf made the irrevocable decision to tease them into thinking the war would be the way they wanted it. And, of course, to give them a war based on just the opposite strategy.

Another key factor in the Coalition success was the fact that the air war had gone decisively in favor of the Coalition Forces. In fact, it might be said that the Iraqis surrendered control of the air from the very first few hours of the fighting.

By surrendering their air capabilities, they surrendered their ability to reconnoiter the Coalition Forces. They could not tell where the invading troops actually were, where the tanks were, where *anything* was. By giving up air capability, they gave up their eyes, their ability to gain intelligence about their enemy forces.

And so when the British moved their huge tank forces *away* from the Kuwaiti border and into western Saudi Arabia at the start of the ground war, the Iraqis did not know it. And what was even more important in the crazy world of intelligence and counterintelligence, the British knew they didn't know it.

"We were tuned in to the Iraqi command radio net," said one British officer. "We heard them give the release order to their front-line troops to use chemical weapons against Rhino Force if it crossed the border."

The Iraqis had fallen for the trick and they had sprung the trap! (In the event, incidentally, no chemical weapons were used.)

Schwarzkopf's "Hail Mary" attack—named after the desperation pass in the last seconds of any football game in which the quarterback simply lobs the ball into the end zone along with a prayer—the circling and flanking of the Coalition ground forces and then the penetrating, dividing, and smashing of the Republican Guard against the Euphrates River and marshes to the northeast of Kuwait City, worked absolutely and totally. To the detriment of the Iraqi army.

Along the three-hundred-mile front of the Saudi-Iraqi border the enemy was surrendering in droves. Columns of them were marching across the desert toward the allies, tanks and bunkers abandoned after weeks of relentless pounding.

"It's the most incredible thing I've ever seen," said Colonel Ron Rokos, commander of the 2nd Brigade of the 82nd Airborne Division. "Every soldier I saw surrendered."

Some prisoners even pointed out nearby mine fields and pinpointed Iraqi units for the Coalition Forces.

"There's nothing to this," said one amazed American marine. "It's like a nature hike. They jump up like squirrels to surrender."

"I hate to say it," another mused, "but once we got rolling, it was like a training exercise with the live people running around. Our training exercises are a lot harder."

General Michel Roquejeoffre, overall commander of all French forces in the Persian Gulf, was out on a survey of his forces in a Puma helicopter when he saw four Iraqi soldiers prostrate on the ground.

"If someone is wounded we must pick him up," said the general as he ordered his pilot to land. "If they are dead we can't leave them like that."

One American pilot who was forced to eject and land in the desert was soon surrounded by dozens of Iraqi troops trying to surrender to him. Another American army jeep became separated from its column and got stuck in the mud. An Iraqi tank appeared, towed the jeep out, and then surrendered to the Americans.

A number of Iraqi soldiers tried to surrender to a drone—a plane operated under remote control many miles away—after it landed in the sand. The camera in the nose cone was still working. Its operator back in Saudi Arabia was startled to see the Iraqis waving white flags at him through the lens of the camera.

"Was it a rout? You're damned right it was a rout," said Brigadier General Richard Neal, Operation Desert Storm's spokesperson in Riyadh—the voice of General Schwarzkopf.

"It was a rout caused by aggressive U.S. and Coalition actions."

"It takes two sides to fight a war," said a military analyst named Jeff Record. "In this war, the opposing side turned into a no-show."

The placement of division after division of elite Republican Guard troops along the Saudi-Kuwaiti border was reminiscent of World War I trench warfare—hardly the moves of a modern military tactician.

"[Saddam Hussein] in fact set them up for the kill," said Colonel Tom Lennon, commander of the 48th Tactical Fighter Wing—whose F-111 fighter bombers destroyed more than 750 tanks in air attacks.

Meanwhile, Schwarzkopf was euphoric. All along he had been agonizing about sending his troops into battle. "I don't want my troops to die, I don't want my troops to be maimed," he had said several times before the ground war began. He was, as H-Hour for the ground war drew near, "a little jumpy," in the estimate of an aide.

In fact, Schwarzkopf had predicted that—if all went well— the ground campaign would last between eight and sixteen days. Just to be on the safe side, he had built up stockpiles for enough supplies to last sixty days. And here it was, all wrapped up in four days!

"We couldn't believe the early reports," one Pentagon general said. "We all thought there must have been a communications failure and then we began to realize it was real."

Schwarzkopf was hearing nothing but glowing reports that kept coming in to him.

"We killed 630 tanks and only lost four tanks and two Bradleys," said General Ronald Griffith, commander of the American 1st Division, which led the flanking attack against the elite Iraqi troops. "I don't think there is any doubt that we destroyed the Republican Guard."

Griffith had watched most of the battle from his Blackhawk command helicopter. "It was most probably the most powerful armored division on the move in history. This is going to go down as one of the great armored campaigns."

Schwarzkopf utilized four essential elements of maneuver

warfare in the successful liberation of Kuwait: surprise, strength, envelopment, and deception. This was classic stuff, the same elements used in victory by Eisenhower, Rommel, Patton, Lee, and even Hannibal.

All in all, it was The Bear who dominated the war by sheer force of personality, plus his brilliant strategy of the flanking maneuver that wrapped up the Iraqi armed force into a neat package and collapsed it under the weight of the bombing and the speed of the later encircling assault.

Down the line of command, Schwarzkopf and Powell could see the combined efforts paying off. There would be textbooks written about Marine Lieutenant General Walter Boomer, for example, who punched his army through dense Iraqi fortifications and raced to Kuwait City, while a potential amphibious force kept Iraqi troops pinned to the Kuwaiti coast, watching the horizon for the landing that never developed.

"He knew the art of war damn well," said Lieutenant General William Yarborough, a retired army veteran of special operations and airborne campaigns. "His place in history is assured. The fact there wasn't a hell of a lot of opposition doesn't mean there couldn't have been."

"General Schwarzkopf followed the classic principle of modern warfare," said Anthony Farra-Hockley, a retired British general. "First win the air battle." Accomplishing that gave the Coalition Forces full view of Iraqi deployments while leaving the enemy blind to Coalition maneuvers.

Lieutenant General Sir Peter de la Billiere, the British commander in the Persian Gulf, described Schwarzkopf's overall operation as "possibly the most complete victory in the history of war."

About Schwarzkopf, he said: "It is his brilliance, his leadership, his drive, his determination—and I have to say it occasionally—his rudeness that's got things done and gotten done so damned efficiently and helped us and enabled us to win this war. So General Schwarzkopf is indeed the man of the match."

De la Billiere went on to say, "Let us remember they [the Iraqis] were the fourth largest army in the world and they were defeated in one hundred hours, which is not bad going." He pointed out that he was taking home, alive and well, nearly all of the servicemen and women sent into Desert Storm from Britain.

"I draw the greatest satisfaction from the small number of casualties. If I take away one memory of this operation, it will be the fact that so much has been achieved with so few lives lost."

He gave credit to the Coalition's "meticulously planned" campaign designed to soften up the battlefield with the allies' vastly superior air power before deploying ground forces.

"This was used with great strategic precision to ensure that not only was the battlefield prepared before the land forces went in, but also the whole of the military machine in Iraq was degraded to the point where it could not reinforce or support the battlefield. Furthermore, the air power was finally used in great concentration to prepare the battlefield itself and soften up the area by attriting the units, the tanks, the armored personnel carriers, the artillery down to a level where, provided we concentrated, we could overwhelm him without much difficulty."

But it was Schwarzkopf and Powell—the two military men who drew up, developed, and brought to final fruition the detailed plan of Operation Desert Storm—who deserved the lion's share of the adulation of the public. Because Schwarzkopf was in the public eye from the beginning, he became the high-profile symbol of Desert Shield and Desert Storm.

"Tough-guy, bogey-man, and television star," one English journalist wrote about him. "He may not have frightened us, but, by God, he frightened the enemy.... [He was a] 1950s comic book character come to life. But behind the beef (one reporter described him as 'ox-like') was a brain. We learnt of his intellect, his command of foreign languages, his coolness and heroism in a Vietnam minefield. He would relax by performing magic tricks for his children or by listening to tape recordings of duck calls."

But the most telling analysis of Schwarzkopf's strategy came later: "The projection of General [H. Norman] Schwarzkopf as a 'kick-ass' hard man can itself now be seen as part of the huge deception plan. The six foot four inch, eighteen-stone general accused Saddam of wanting a 'slugfest.' Instead of an

arm-wrestling match, Schwarzkopf delivered a classic performance of the operational art of war propelled by brain more
than muscle, with astonishingly light casualties on the allied
side.''

To lull the enemy, ''Schwarzkopf had to play the bruiser.
He [later] thanked reporters for helping to compound the fluff,
'giving us credit for a whole lot more weaponry than we had.' ''

It was General Colin L. Powell, Chairman of the Joint Chiefs
of Staff, who called his colleague General H. Norman Schwarzkopf ''a statesman who understands the political and diplomatic
dimensions of a national security issue.'' He was, Powell said,
''the kind of general that President Lincoln searched for
throughout most of the Civil War.''

And it was First Lady Barbara Bush who saw Schwarzkopf
as a ''cross between George Patton and Fuzzy Bear.''

The United States Senate felt a great deal of warmth toward
not only General Schwarzkopf but his direct superior, General
Powell. In order to make its gratitude known to its two favorite
generals, the Senate approved the awarding of Congressional
Gold Medals to Powell as Chairman of the Joint Chiefs of Staff
and to Schwarzkopf as commander of Operation Desert Storm
for their leadership in the Persian Gulf War.

By a voice vote, the Senate agreed to the awarding of the
gold medals to the generals and to the minting of bronze copies
that would be put on public sale as commemorative coins.

As for Schwarzkopf, his only comment at the ending of the
war was: ''I want to come home and be with my family, then
go out with all my buddies and shoot sporting clays and then
probably go fishing.''

''You're going to come home such a hero,'' Barbara Walters
told him.

Schwarzkopf corrected her. ''But I'm not a hero, and that's
important. . . . It doesn't take a hero to order men into battle.
It takes a hero to be one of those men that goes into battle.
. . . Those are the people that are the heroes. Those are the
people that should receive the adulation.''

Later he paused to talk briefly about military men and
women—and especially, and most important, about the families of military men and women.

"The military family is just as much of a hero as the troops are," he said, "and people don't realize it. But . . . if you love a soldier, if you love a sailor, if you love a marine, if you love an airman, you're going to sacrifice a lot. People don't realize how much they sacrifice."

He paused a moment, and then smiled. "So, all I want to say to the families is this: 'Thanks for loving us.'"

FROM PERSONAL JOURNALS TO BLACKLY HUMOROUS ACCOUNTS

VIETNAM

DISPATCHES, Michael Herr
                          01976-0/$4.50 US/$5.95 Can
"I believe it may be the best personal journal about war, any war, that any writer has ever accomplished."
                    —Robert Stone, *Chicago Tribune*

M, John Sack
                          69866-8/$3.95 US/$4.95 Can
"A gripping and honest account, compassionate and rich, colorful and blackly comic."
                    —*The New York Times*

ONE BUGLE, NO DRUMS, Charles Durden
                          69260-0/$4.95 US/$5.95 Can
"The funniest, ghastliest military scenes put to paper since Joseph Heller wrote *Catch-22*"
                    —*Newsweek*

AMERICAN BOYS, Steven Phillip Smith
                          67934-5/$4.50 US/$5.95 Can
"The best novel I've come across on the war in Vietnam"
                    —Norman Mailer

WORLD WAR II
Edwin P. Hoyt

STORM OVER THE GILBERTS: 63651-4/$3.50 US/$4.50 Can
War in the Central Pacific: 1943
The dramatic reconstruction of the bloody battle over the Japanese-held Gilbert Islands.

CLOSING THE CIRCLE: 67983-8/$3.50 US/$4.95 Can
War in the Pacific: 1945
A behind-the-scenes look at the military and political moves drawn from official American and Japanese sources.

McCAMPBELL'S HEROES   68841-7/$3.95 US/$5.75 Can
A stirring account of the daring fighter pilots, led by Captain David McCampbell, of Air Group Fifteen.

LEYTE GULF   75408-8/$3.50 US/$4.50 Can
The Death of the Princeton
The true story of a bomb-torn American aircraft carrier fighting a courageous battle for survival!

WAR IN THE PACIFIC: TRIUMPH OF JAPAN
        75792-3/$4.50 US/$5.50 Can

WAR IN THE PACIFIC: STIRRINGS   75793-1/$3.95 US/$4.95 Can

THE JUNGLES OF NEW GUINEA   75750-8/$4.95 US/$5.95 Can